Accounting

Book 1

John Taylor
Stephen Peltier - C.P.A., M.S.

Express Publishing

Scope and Sequence

Unit	Topic	Reading context	Vocabulary	Function
1	Jobs in Accounting	Advertisement	back-office, bookkeeper, budget analysis, client, CPA, file clerk, firm, internal auditor, tax accountant, trainee	Introducing yourself
2	Numbers	Chart	add, and, divided by, equals, hundred, is, less, minus, multiplied by, over, plus, subtract, times	Expressing confusion
3	Office Materials	Invoice	binder, bulletin board, cubicle divider, desk lamp, dry eraser, file cabinet, note pad, paper clip, stapler, whiteboard	Apologizing to a client
4	Electronic Tools	Proposal	calculator, CD/DVD drive, copier, desktop computer, fax machine, flash drive, landline telephone, laptop computer, mobile telephone, printer	Asking about purpose
5	Bookkeeping Cycle	Blog	accounting software, adjusted trial balance, credit card statement, end-of-period procedure, fiscal year, payroll master file, payroll, purchase invoice, source document, time card, transaction	Confirming information
6	GAAP and IASB	Magazine Article	broad-scale uniformity, consistent, disclosure, FASB, governing body, IASB, principles-based approach, rules-based approach	Describing pros and cons
7	Income Statements	Income Statement / Magazine	general and administrative expenses, gross margin, income statement, net income, operating margin, P&L, sales revenue, sell, tax	Avoiding distractions
8	Balance Sheets	Balance Sheet / Magazine	accounts payable, accounts receivable, asset, balance sheet, cash, debt, fixed asset, inventory, liability, owner's equity, sum	Giving bad news
9	Cash Flow Statements	Cash Flow Statement / Journal Article	cash distribution, cash flow, cumulative, dividend, financing activity, generate, inflow, outflow, proceeds, stockholder	Confirming meaning
10	Describing Change	Report	decline, dramatically, hover, plummet, recover, sharply, slightly, stabilize, steadily	Making a prediction
11	Gleaning Info from Financial Statements	Email	assess, eat away at, factor, interpret, return on equity, return on sales, thin, uncollectable, year-over-year growth rate	Describing speed of work
12	Overdrafts	Bank Notice	cash a check, charge, compensate, inform, overdraft, transfer, upcoming, withdrawal	Offering services
13	Costs	Magazine Article	below cost, cost-plus method, dumping, markup, out of business, predatory, sales price, sue	Reacting to expected news
14	Taxes	Advertisement	corporate tax, excise tax, file, inheritance tax, IRS, property tax, sales tax, specialize, tax form, value-added tax	Asking for information
15	Depreciation	Memo	accelerated depreciation, depreciable asset, depreciation, depreciation methods, depreciation schedule, obsolescence, recovery period, salvage value, straight-line depreciation, tangible asset, wear and tear	Agreeing with a suggestion

Table of Contents

Unit 1 – Jobs in Accounting 4

Unit 2 – Numbers 6

Unit 3 – Office Materials 8

Unit 4 – Electronic Tools 10

Unit 5 – Bookkeeping Cycle 12

Unit 6 – GAAP and IASB 14

Unit 7 – Income Statements 16

Unit 8 – Balance Sheets 18

Unit 9 – Cash Flow Statements 20

Unit 10 – Describing Change 22

Unit 11 – Gleaning Information from Financial Statements 24

Unit 12 – Overdrafts 26

Unit 13 – Costs 28

Unit 14 – Taxes 30

Unit 15 – Depreciation 32

Glossary 34

1 Jobs in Accounting

Get ready!

1 Before you read the passage, talk about these questions.

1. What jobs do accountants do?
2. What are the educational requirements for accountants?

tax accountants

back-office

Accounting is a GREAT career choice!

There are many jobs available for accountants. Here are a few:

- **Bookkeepers** work in a company's **back-office**. They record everything the organization earns or spends.
- **Tax Accountants** help their **clients** fill out tax returns.
- **Internal Auditors** check their employer's records for accuracy.
- **Budget Analysts** manage a company's financial plans.
- **Management Accountants** are business supervisors. They study business operations and help maximize profits.
- **Financial Advisors** help people make smart investments.

The highest-paying positions require a **CPA** license. But jobs are also available for students. Many **firms** hire them as **trainees** or **file clerks**.

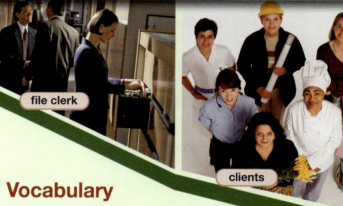
file clerk • clients

Reading

2 Read the advertisement from a business college. Then, choose the correct answers.

1. What is the advertisement mainly about?
    A a new record keeping method
    B how to invest wisely
    C steps to becoming a CPA
    D different accounting jobs

2. People discuss investments with _____.
    A bookkeepers   C financial advisors
    B trainees   D file clerks

3. What can be inferred about file clerks?
    A They work as volunteers.
    B They train for at least a year.
    C They are not required to have CPA licenses.
    D They have one of the highest-paying positions.

Vocabulary

3 Match the words or phrases (1-5) with the definitions (A-E).

1 __ budget analyst   4 __ internal auditor
2 __ bookkeeper   5 __ tax accountant
3 __ trainee

A a person who fills out tax forms
B a person who records transactions
C a person who reviews financial plans
D a person who is learning a new job
E a person who checks records for accuracy

4

④ **Fill in the blanks with the correct words or phrases from the word bank.**

word BANK

back-office   clients   file clerk   firm   CPA

1. Steve needs a _____ license to get a higher-paying job.
2. John is in accounting school. He also works as a _____.
3. Most bookkeepers work in the _____.
4. Accountants who advertise on TV get more _____.
5. Some accountants work alone. Others work for a _____.

⑤ 🎧 **Listen and read the advertisement again. What area does a management accountant specialize in?**

Listening

⑥ 🎧 **Listen to a conversation between an accountant and a supervisor. Mark the following statements as true (T) or false (F).**

1. __ The man is nervous about working for the company.
2. __ The man was hired as an internal auditor.
3. __ The bookkeepers work in the back-office.

⑦ 🎧 **Listen again and complete the conversation.**

Accountant:	Hello. You 1 _____ _____ Ms. Davenport. I'm Jason Williams.
Supervisor:	Jason! Hi. How are you?
Accountant:	Great, thanks. I'm really 2 _____ to start working with your firm.
Supervisor:	Good. We're glad to have you. Let me show you 3 _____. Obviously, this is the 4 _____ - _____.
Accountant:	This is where I'll be working, right?
Supervisor:	That's 5 _____. All the bookkeepers work here.
Accountant:	So can I get started now?
Supervisor:	Well, first you need to 6 _____ _____ with the accounting manager. I'll introduce you.

Speaking

⑧ **With a partner, act out the roles below based on Task 7. Then switch roles.**

USE LANGUAGE SUCH AS:
You must be ... I'm ...
Let me show you around.
You need to check in with ...

Student A: It's your first day as an accountant. Talk to Student B about:
- how you feel
- where you will work
- checking in

Student B: You are a senior accountant. Answer Student A's questions.

Writing

⑨ **Use the conversation from Task 8 to fill out the new employee form. Make up a name for the employee.**

BY THE NUMBERS ACCOUNTING FIRM

New Employee Information

Employee Name: _____

Position: _____

Responsibilities: _____

5

2 Numbers

How do they say it?

Symbol	Interpretation	Example	
=	is, equals	1/2 = 0.5	One-half equals point five.
+	and, plus, add	a + b = c	A plus B equals C.
−	minus, less, subtract	a − b = c	A less B equals C.
×	times, multiplied by	a x b = c	A times B equals C.
÷ or /	over, divided by	a ÷ b = c or a / b = c	A over B equals C.
1300	one thousand three hundred or thirteen **hundred**		The company has thirteen hundred dollars in the bank.

Get Ready!

1 Before you read the chart, talk about these questions.

1. How do you say symbols like = and ÷ ?
2. What are some of the ways to say big numbers?

Reading

2 Read the chart. Then, mark the following statements as true (T) or false (F).

1. _T_ Five less four means the same thing as five minus four.
2. _F_ Five times three equals five plus three.
3. _T_ Seven over three equals seven divided by three.

Vocabulary

3 Fill in the blanks with the correct words from the word bank.

word BANK

times   minus   and   hundred   add   is

1. Eight _times_ two is sixteen.
2. Nine and three _is_ twelve.
3. Twenty _minus_ six equals fourteen.
4. One thousand plus five hundred is fifteen _hundred_.
5. To get seven, _add_ two and five.
6. Eighteen _and_ two is twenty.

4 Read the sentences and choose the correct words.

1. Seven **plus / divided by** two is nine.
2. Nineteen **over / less** eight equals eleven.
3. Start with seventeen. **Subtract / Add** three. This equals fourteen.
4. Four **multiplied by / divided by** two is eight.
5. Ten **over / plus** five equals two.
6. Sixteen **less / divided by** four equals four.
7. Five plus eight **equals / over** thirteen.

5 🎧 Listen and read the chart again. What is another way to say the symbol 'and'?

Listening

6 🎧 Listen to a conversation between two accountants. Choose the correct answers.

1. What is the dialogue mostly about?
   - A audit results
   - B a mathematical error
   - C subtracting numbers
   - D accounting methods

2. The woman divided when she should have _____.
   - A added
   - B subtracted
   - C copied
   - D multiplied

7 🎧 Listen again and complete the conversation.

Accountant 1:	Don, could you look at this for me?
Accountant 2:	Sure, what is it?
Accountant 1:	Well, I checked these numbers twice, but they still 1 _are_ wrong. I'm not sure why.
Accountant 2:	Let's see ... Three thousand five hundred 2 _divided_ seven hundred is five.
Accountant 1:	Right. And then I 3 _mupl_ each entry by five.
Accountant 2:	Oh, I see the 4 _error_. You weren't 5 _supposed to_ divide thirty-five hundred by seven hundred.
Accountant 1:	Are you 6 _sure_?
Accountant 2:	Yes. You need to multiply them.

Speaking

8 With a partner, act out the roles below based on Task 7. Then switch roles.

USE LANGUAGE SUCH AS:
Could you look at this for me?
I'm not sure why.
I see the problem.

Student A: You are having trouble with an accounting task. Ask Student B about:
- your work
- errors
- solutions

Student B: You are an accountant. Answer Student A's questions.

Writing

9 Use the chart and the conversation from Task 8 to complete the email. Make up names for both accounts.

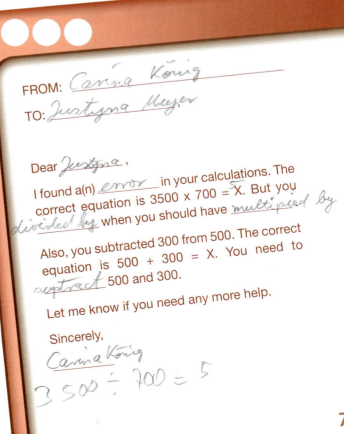

3 Office Materials

Date	Your Order #	Our Order #	Sales Rep	Ship Via	Terms	Tax ID
2010.10.30	626	100967.626	DF	Ultimate Transit	2/10 n30	229887466

Quantity	Description	Unit Price	Total
500	Paper Clips	$0.02	$10.00
20	Stapler	$15.00	$300.00
30	Desk Lamp	$25.00	$750.00
4	Bulletin Board	$10.00	$40.00
10	File Cabinet	$99.00	$990.00
5	Whiteboard	$12.00	$60.00
10	Dry Eraser	$3.00	$30.00
250	Binder	$1.00	$250.00
50	Note Pad	$2.00	$100.00
10	Cubicle Divider	$120.00	$1200.00
	Subtotal		$3730.00
	Tax (10%)		$373.00
	Shipping		$150.00
	Balance Due		$4253.00

Mega-Office Supply provides superior products and customer service. Please let us know immediately if you are not completely satisfied with your order.

Get Ready!

1 Before you read the passage, talk about these questions.

1. What supplies do offices need?
2. How much do office supplies cost?

Reading

2 Read the invoice from an office supply company. Then, mark the following statements as true (T) or false (F).

1. __ One bulletin board costs more than one stapler.
2. __ The customer is required to pay a ten-percent tax.
3. __ The customer will pick up the order in person.

Vocabulary

3 Match the words or phrases (1-6) with the definitions (A-F).

1. __ note pad
2. __ desk lamp
3. __ paper clip
4. __ cubicle divider
5. __ binder
6. __ bulletin board

A a small object that holds papers together
B a book of blank paper used for writing
C thin barriers that divide office space
D a device that illuminates a work space
E a wall panel that people post messages on
F a notebook with rings or clamps to hold paper

4 Read the sentence pairs. Choose which word or phrase best fits each blank.

1 file cabinet / white board
   A Update the records, then put them in the _____.
   B Start the meeting by writing your name on the _____.

2 stapler / dry eraser
   A She used the _____ to clear the white board.
   B The papers fell apart. My _____ must be broken.

5 🎧 Listen and read the invoice again. What is the cost of two staplers, ten note pads, fifty binders and a desk lamp, plus tax?

Listening

6 🎧 Listen to a conversation between a bookkeeper and a customer service representative. Choose the correct answers.

1 What is the dialogue mostly about?
   A placing an order   C an order error
   B broken merchandise D shipping times

2 What will the man likely do next?
   A give the woman a refund
   B ask for more information
   C ask the woman to return the lamps
   D complete the woman's order

7 🎧 Listen again and complete the conversation.

Representative:	Mega-Office Supply. How may I help you?
Bookkeeper:	Hi. This is Stacy from Equity Accountants. There's a problem with 1 _____ #626.
Representative:	Sorry to 2 _____ that. What's the problem?
Bookkeeper:	You 3 _____ thirteen desk lamps; but we ordered thirty.
Representative:	I'm sorry, I didn't quite 4 _____ that. What did you say?
Bookkeeper:	I said we 5 _____ thirteen desk lamps; but we ordered thirty.
Representative:	I see. Well, I 6 _____ for the error. We'll ship the rest today.
Bookkeeper:	Thank you!

Speaking

8 With a partner, act out the roles below based on Task 7. Then switch roles.

USE LANGUAGE SUCH AS:
There's a problem with ...
You sent ... but we ordered ...
I apologize for the error. We'll ...

Student A: You are calling an office supply company. Talk to Student B about:
- an error
- what you ordered
- what you received

Student B: You work at an office supply company. Answer Student A's questions.

Writing

9 Use the conversation from Task 8 to complete the packing slip.

Mega OFFICE SUPPLY

Original order: _____
Units shipped: _____

Number of missing units: _____

Please accept our apology for our error on your last order.

Thank you for your patience.

Sincerely,

_____,
President, Mega-Office Supply

4 Electronic Tools

Get Ready!

1 Before you read the passage, talk about these questions.

1. What electronic devices do accountants use?
2. What do they use them for?

Mr. Wenton,

We reviewed your business plan. Your ideas are very realistic. We are happy to help you start your company. Here is a list of electronic devices that you need:

- Laptop Computer
- Desktop Computer with CD/DVD drive
- Flash drives
- Printer
- Copier
- Fax machine
- Calculator
- Landline telephone
- Mobile telephone
- Desk lamps

Mega-Office Supply sells these items. They offer free delivery in town. With your permission, we can place the order. Delivery takes one week on most items. The computers, printer, and copier may take longer.

Cordially,
Timothy Johnson and Rebecca Meyers
Johnson-Meyers Consulting, LLC

Reading

2 Read the proposal from a consulting company. Then, choose the correct answers.

1. What is the passage mainly about?
   A. delivering office supplies
   B. replacing broken equipment
   C. requesting newer equipment
   D. suggesting electronic equipment

2. Which of the following may be delivered late?
   A. a calculator   C. a copier
   B. flash drives   D. a fax machine

3. What can be inferred about Mr. Wenton?
   A. He has written many business plans.
   B. He already has a desktop computer.
   C. He will not talk to the supply company personally.
   D. He worked with the consulting company in the past.

Vocabulary

3 Match the words (1-5) with the definitions (A-E).

1. ___ laptop computer
2. ___ CD/DVD drive
3. ___ landline telephone
4. ___ calculator
5. ___ printer

A. a machine that converts computer documents into paper documents
B. a portable electronic device that performs various tasks
C. a device that is only used for mathematical operations
D. an optical disc drive
E. a device used to talk to people over long distances

④ **Fill in the blanks with the correct words or phrases from the word bank.**

word BANK

desktop computer   flash drives   copier
    mobile telephone   fax machine

1. Jack needs a _____ to access the Internet from his office.
2. _____ are the most convenient storage devices.
3. Paula heard her _____ ringing in her pocket.
4. George can't duplicate documents because his _____ broke.
5. A _____ is the most efficient way to scan and send documents.

⑤ 🎧 **Listen and read the proposal again. What do the advisers think about Mr Wenton's plans?**

Listening

⑥ 🎧 **Listen to a conversation between an accountant and a consultant. Mark the following statements as true (T) or false (F).**

1. ___ The man thinks no one uses drives.
2. ___ The woman recommends flash drives.
3. ___ The man accepts all of the woman's recommendations

⑦ 🎧 **Listen again and complete the conversation.**

Accountant:	Thanks for the 1 _____ . They all look good except for one.
Consultant:	2 _____ one is that?
Accountant:	It's the CD/DVD drive. 3 _____ _____ why do I need a CD/DVD drive?
Consultant:	Well, you may want to view and store 4 _____ files or install large applications.
Accountant:	Hmm ... I don't know 5 _____ that still uses those.
Consultant:	OK. You could just 6 _____ _____ a flash drive.
Accountant:	Yes. I think most people use flash drives.
Consultant:	That's true, but some people still use CDs/DVDs.

Speaking

⑧ **With a partner, act out the roles below based on Task 7. Then switch roles.**

> **USE LANGUAGE SUCH AS:**
> *Thanks for the recommendations.*
> *They look good except ...*
> *You could just use ...*

Student A: You are starting a business. Talk to Student B about:
- necessary equipment
- common devices

Student B: You are a consultant. Answer Student A's questions.

Writing

⑨ **Use the proposal and the conversation from Task 8 to complete the order.**

Mega OFFICE SUPPLY — ORDER FOR DELIVERY

One _____ _____
One desktop computer with a _____ drive
One _____
One _____ machine
One _____ phone
One _____

11

5 Bookkeeping Cycle

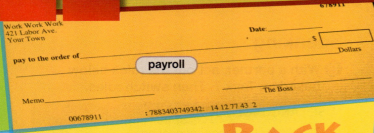

GETTING BACK TO BASICS

Let's review the basic bookkeeping cycle. No matter what type of organization you work in, there are six steps.

1. Gather **source documents** for all **transactions**. These include:
   - Purchase invoices
   - Payroll Master Files
   - Time cards
   - Credit card statements

2. Analyze the financial effect of every transaction. Typical transactions include:
   - **Payroll**
   - Sales
   - Purchases

3. Record financial effects in a journal. Then post them in the **accounting software**.

4. Perform **end-of-period procedures**:
   - Count inventory
   - Check for errors in classification
   - Adjust for errors

5. Prepare an **adjusted trial balance**.

6. Close the books at the end of every **fiscal year**.

Get Ready!

❶ Before you read the passage, talk about these questions.

1. What are the basic tasks in bookkeeping?
2. What are some of the documents that they use?

Reading

❷ Read the entry on a bookkeeper's blog. Then, choose the correct answers.

1. What is the passage mainly about?
   A end-of-period procedures
   B minimizing financial effects
   C steps in the bookkeeping cycle
   D how to gather source documents

2. According to the passage, which is NOT a source document?
   A credit card statement
   B purchase invoice
   C accounting software
   D payroll master files

3. What is true according to the passage?
   A Every organization follows a different bookkeeping cycle.
   B Financial effects are recorded in two different places.
   C Adjusted trial balances carry over to the next fiscal year.
   D Accounting software creates most source documents.

Vocabulary

❸ Match the words (1-6) with the definitions (A-F).

1 __ source documents
2 __ transaction
3 __ credit card slip
4 __ purchase invoice
5 __ payroll master file
6 __ accounting software

A a purchase, sale, or payment
B a receipt for a credit card purchase
C a file containing employee's salary information
D a document requesting payment for a purchase
E a computer program that organizes financial data
F documents from various financial transactions

❹ **Fill in the blanks with the correct words or phrases from the word bank.**

word BANK

time card   adjusted trial balance   fiscal year
payroll   end-of-period procedures

1 Jack made a few errors while preparing the _____ .
2 In Canada, the _____ goes from April to March.
3 Perform _____ before opening books for the new period.
4 _____ is one of the most predictable business expenses.
5 Tim didn't clock in, so his _____ is short eight hours.

❺ 🎧 Listen and read the bookkeeper's blog again. At which step are classification mistakes corrected?

Listening

❻ 🎧 Listen to a conversation between a junior accountant and a senior accountant. Mark the following statements as true (T) or false (F).

1 __ The man maintains the accounting software.
2 __ The woman will not collect the source documents.
3 __ The department managers supply source documents weekly.

❼ 🎧 **Listen again and complete the conversation.**

Accountant 1:	Do you have a 1 _____ , Mr. Smith?
Accountant 2:	Certainly, Nancy. What can I help you with?
Accountant 1:	One question — how do I collect the 2 _____ _____ ?
Accountant 2:	Actually, you don't collect them.
Accountant 1:	Really? How do I 3 _____ _____ ?
Accountant 2:	The 4 _____ managers give them to you at the end of every month.
Accountant 1:	Ah, I see. So then I just 5 _____ the data in the accounting software?
Accountant 2:	That's right. 6 _____ the data from the source documents in the accounting software.

Speaking

❽ **With a partner, act out the roles below based on Task 7. Then switch roles.**

> **USE LANGUAGE SUCH AS:**
> Do you have a moment?
> How do I ...?
> So then I just ...?

Student A: You are a new accountant. Talk to Student B about:
• gathering documents
• recording data

Student B: You are a senior accountant. Answer Student A's questions.

Writing

❾ **Use the conversation from Task 8 to fill out the accountant's notes.**

Duties/Frequency

Department managers
_____
_____

Accountants:
_____

6 GAAP and IASB

Businesses exchange information, therefore companies must have **broad-scale uniformity** in their records. Information must stay **consistent**.

U.S.A. — Generally Accepted Accounting Principles (GAAP)

In the USA, the Financial Accounting Standards Board (**FASB**) has a system. It's called Generally Accepted Accounting Principles (GAAP). GAAP is a **rules-based approach**. It creates rules for **disclosure**.

EUROPE — International Accounting Standards Board (IASB)

In Europe, there is another **governing body**. It's called the International Accounting Standards Board (**IASB**). It uses a **principles-based approach**. It describes general accounting principles. Accountants use these as a guide. It shows them how to record financial transactions and include proper disclosure in financial statements.

Companies can decide which approach to use. Many choose both.

Get Ready!

1 Before you read the passage, talk about these questions.

1. What are some rules that accountants have to follow?
2. How do accounting rules change in different parts of the world?

Reading

2 Read the magazine article. Then, mark the following statements as true (T) or false (F).

1. ___ Europe and the United States have different accounting standards.
2. ___ The FASB creates standardized rules for the governing bodies.
3. ___ IASB accounting standards follow a principles-based approach.

Vocabulary

3 Write a word that is similar in meaning to the underlined part.

1. The company follows both the FASB and the <u>European body that sets accounting standards</u>. _ _ _ _
2. FASB is the governing body that establishes <u>American accounting standards</u>. _ _ _ _
3. Accounting records must be <u>the same across numerous samples</u>. _ _ n _ s _ _ _ _ t
4. American accounting standards include rules for <u>giving out financial information</u>. _ i _ c _ _ s _ _ _

4 Fill in the blanks with the correct words or phrases from the word bank.

WORD BANK

rules-based approach   broad-scale uniformity   FASB
principles-based approach   governing bodies

1. GAAP is a _____ .
2. _____ design accounting standards.
3. Most European companies follow a _____ .
4. _____ is the organization that makes accounting rules in America.
5. Accounting standards provide _____ among organizations.

5 🎧 Listen and read the article again. Which standard do the majority of companies use?

Listening

6 🎧 Listen to a conversation between two accountants. Choose the correct answers.

1. What is the dialogue mostly about?
   A the flexibility of IASB
   B advantages of using GAAP
   C which accounting standards to use
   D businesses in Europe and the USA

2. The accountants use both standards because they
   A have clients in Europe and the USA.
   B want to determine which is better.
   C don't want to be inconsistent.
   D have clients that requested it.

7 🎧 Listen again and complete the conversation.

Accountant 1: Did you read the **1** _____ this morning?
Accountant 2: You mean the one that says we have to follow both GAAP and IASB?
Accountant 1: Yes. Why do we have to follow both?
Accountant 2: Well, both have **2** _____ and disadvantages.
Accountant 1: Like what?
Accountant 2: GAAP has **3** _____ instructions. But it is restrictive. IASB is **4** _____ . But it can be inconsistent.
Accountant 1: Why not just pick one **5** _____ to use?
Accountant 2: Well, we have clients in both the USA and Europe. It's better to use both **6** _____ that they are familiar with.

Speaking

8 With a partner, act out the roles below based on Task 7. Then switch roles.

USE LANGUAGE SUCH AS:
Did you read the ...?
Why do we have to ...?
GAAP has ... But it's also ...

Student A: You are an accountant. Talk to Student B about:
- accounting standards
- advantages of each
- disadvantages of each

Student B: You are an accountant. Answer Student A's questions.

Writing

9 Use the conversation from Task 8 to fill out the accountant's notes.

Accounting Standards

	GAAP	IASB
Advantages		
Disadvantages		
Primarily used in		

7 Income Statements

Getting to the Bottom Line

Most people know that the term "bottom line" means "the most important thing." But it's also an accounting term. It refers to the bottom line of an **income statement**. An income statement is also called a **P & L**. That means "profit and loss." A P & L statement shows a summary of a company's financial transactions over a period of time.

It starts with **sales revenue**. This is the money a company gets from **selling** goods. The cost of those goods is deducted from the revenue. Next the **general and administrative expenses** are deducted. Finally, **taxes** are subtracted.

The number that remains on the bottom line is called **net income**. This amount is the company's bottom line.

Income Statement

	2010	2011
Sales Revenue	700,000	500,000
Less Cost of Goods Sold	500,000	500,000
Gross Margin	**200,000**	**0**
Less General and Administrative Expenses	90,000	90,000
Operating Margin	**110,000**	**(90,000)**
Less Taxes	7,000	5,000
Net Income	**103,000**	**(95,000)**

Get Ready!

1 Before you read the passage, talk about these questions.

1 What information goes on income statements?
2 How do companies use income statements?

Reading

2 Read the income statement and magazine article. Then, mark the following statements as true (T) or false (F).

1 __ "Bottom line" means net income.
2 __ Operating margin minus taxes is gross margin.
3 __ P & L statements show information from a period of time.

Vocabulary

3 Match the words or phrases (1-5) with the definitions (A-E).

1 __ gross margin   4 __ P & L
2 __ sales revenue   5 __ general and administrative expenses
3 __ taxes

A a statement showing financial information for a certain period
B money that is paid to a government
C the costs associated with organizing and running a business
D an amount that is calculated by subtracting cost of goods sold
E the money that is received from selling goods or services

4 Fill in the blanks with the correct words or phrases: *operating margin*, *income statement*, *net income*, *selling*.

1 Subtract taxes from the _____ to find net income.
2 _____ is the act of exchanging goods for money.
3 _____ is the amount of money retained after all expenses
4 A(n) _____ is a document showing how much money was made.

5 🎧 Listen and read the income statement and article again. What is deducted from sales revenue to show the bottom line?

Listening

6 🎧 Listen to a conversation between two accountants. Choose the correct answers.

1 What is the dialogue mostly about?
   A an increase in sales revenue
   B a new way to report income
   C a previous year's bottom line
   D a disappointing P & L statement

2 The company's bottom line dropped because
   A sales revenue decreased.
   B cost of goods sold increased.
   C the government raised taxes.
   D there was an error in the P & L.

7 🎧 Listen again and complete the conversation.

A 1: Hi, Peter. Would you like some coffee?
A 2: No thanks. Let's get **1** _____ _____ to business.
A 1: OK. Have you seen the **2** _____ P & L?
A 2: No, I haven't. What's the problem?
A 1: Look at this! Our bottom line has really dropped. Just **3** _____ this to last year.
A 2: I see. Sales revenue is **4** _____ down. But cost of goods sold is the same.
A 1: So, what **5** _____ _____ do?
A 2: Well, first we need to **6** _____ our sales ...

Speaking

8 With a partner, act out the roles below based on Task 7. Then switch roles.

USE LANGUAGE SUCH AS:
Let's get right down to business.
What's the problem?
Our ... has really ...

Student A: You are an accountant. Talk to Student B about:
• a P & L statement
• low/high figures
• what to do about it

Student B: You are an accountant. Answer Student A's questions.

Writing

9 Use the conversation from Task 8 and the income statement to fill out the income statement.

INCOME STATEMENT

	2014	2015
_____	800,000	600,000
Less _____ _____ _____	500,000	500,000
Gross Margin	300,000	_____
Less General and Administrative Expenses	90,000	90,000
Operating Margin	_____	10,000
Less Taxes	10,000	7,000
_____	200,000	_____

8 Balance Sheets

The People's Accountant Explains Balance Sheets

Income statements show financial information over a period of time. Balance sheets, on the other hand, show a company's financial status at a certain moment in time. Let me show you how to read them.

Balance sheets follow this equation:

Assets = Liabilities + Owner's Equity

It's that simple. Assets are what a company owns. Liabilities are what a company owes. Equity is what a company is worth.

Assets include **cash**, **inventory**, **accounts receivable**, and **fixed assets** like land and property. Liabilities include **accounts payable** and **debts**. Owner's equity is the total value of the company.

The **sum** of the assets should be equal to the sum of the liabilities plus the owner's equity.

Balance Sheet
As of July 31st, 2015

Assets		Liabilities	
Cash (bank account)	10,000	Accounts Payable	11,000
Accounts Receivable	15,000	Debts	4,000
Inventory	5,000	Total Liabilities	15,000
Fixed Assets	50,000	Owner's Equity	
		Total Equity	65,000
Total Assets	80,000	Total Liabilities and Equity	80,000

Get Ready!

1 Before you read the passage, talk about these questions.

1. What information goes on a balance sheet?
2. How do companies use balance sheets?

Reading

2 Read the balance sheet and magazine article. Then, choose the correct answers.

1. What is the passage mainly about?
   A. tracking accounts payable and debts
   B. calculating the total value of a company
   C. explaining the information on a balance sheet
   D. understanding the effect liabilities have on equity

2. Which of the following is NOT an asset?
   A. land
   B. equity
   C. inventory
   D. accounts receivable

3. What is true according to the passage?
   A. Equity is what a company owns.
   B. Cash and inventory are fixed assets.
   C. Accounts payable are considered debt.
   D. Total assets equal total liabilities and equity.

Vocabulary

3 Match the words or phases (1-5) with the definitions (A-E).

1. __ balance sheet
2. __ owner's equity
3. __ accounts receivable
4. __ asset
5. __ liability

A. what a company is worth
B. something a company owns
C. a record of money that is owed to a company for past sales
D. an amount of money that a company owes
E. a document showing assets, liabilities, and equity

4 Fill in the blanks with the correct words or phrases from the word bank.

WORD BANK

accounts payable   fixed assets
sum   inventory   debt

1. The company records most purchases in _____.
2. Companies with too much _____ can't get loans.
3. _____ is getting low. Fill out a new purchase order.
4. Add those figures. Then tell me what the _____ is.
5. The company has a lot of _____, including a new warehouse.

5 🎧 Listen and read the balance sheet and article again. What is meant by the term fixed assets?

Listening

6 🎧 Listen to a conversation between two accountants. Mark the following statements as true (T) or false (F).

1. __ The man suggests taking on more debt.
2. __ The company has enough cash to pay its debt.
3. __ The woman says there is an error on the balance sheet.

7 🎧 Listen again and complete the conversation.

A 1: 1 _____ _____, but we have a problem.
A 2: What's that?
A 1: I was looking at this month's balance sheet. Our accounts payable shows that we 2 _____ $15,000.
A 2: Why is that a problem?
A 1: Well, we 3 _____ have $10,000 in the bank.
A 2: I see. We have to 4 _____ some money to pay the difference.
A 1: Isn't it a 5 _____ _____ to take on more debt?
A 2: No. Our accounts receivable shows $15,000. We can use that to 6 _____ _____ some debt next month.

Speaking

8 With a partner, act out the roles below based on Task 7. Then switch roles.

USE LANGUAGE SUCH AS:
I'm afraid I have some bad news.
I was looking at our balance sheet ...
We need to ...

Student A: You are an accountant. Talk to Student B about:
- a balance sheet
- low/high figures
- what to do about it

Student B: You are an accountant. Answer Student A's questions.

Writing

9 Use the conversation from Task 8 to fill out the balance sheet.

Balance Sheet   *As of August 31st, 2015*

Assets		Liabilities	
Cash (bank account)	_____	Accounts _____	_____
Accounts _____	_____		25,000
Inventory	10,000	Total Liabilities	_____
Fixed Assets	100,000	**Owner's Equity**	
		Total Equity	95,000
Total Assets	_____	Total Liabilities and Equity	_____

9 Cash Flow Statements

Get Ready!

1 Before you read the passage, talk about these questions.

1. What is a cash flow statement?
2. What are some of the things that go on a cash flow statement?

Where Did All That Cash Go?

R.H. Benton Enterprises, Inc.
Cash Flow
for Year ending December 31, 2015

Cash flow from Operations	
Cash generated from sales	100,000
Payments to suppliers and employees	(70,000)
Payments on debts	(15,000)
Payments on taxes	(5,000)
Net cash flow from operating activities	10,000
Cash flow from Investing	
Payments for new investments	(9,000)
Dividends received	2,000
Net cash flow from investing	(7,000)
Cash flow from Financing	
Debt increases	4,000
Dividends paid to stockholders	(8,000)
Net cash flow from Financing Activities	(4,000)
Net cash flow	**(1,000)**
Cash balance, beginning of year	4,000
Cash balance, end of year	3,000

Sometimes, an income statement shows huge net income. But the cash flow statement shows negative cash flow. How can this be?

Cash flow statements show the **inflow** and **outflow** of cash. This includes:

- revenues and expenses
- **cash distributions** to owners
- **dividends** paid to **stockholders**
- financing activities

When a sale is made, it often takes months for payment to arrive. A company may have **generated** $500,000 in sales, but only received $100,000 in payment. The income statement counts $500,000 in revenue. But the cash flow statement records only **cumulative** cash — the $100,000 in **proceeds**.

Reading

2 Read the cash flow statement and journal article. Then, mark the following statements as true (T) or false (F).

1. __ Cash flow statements only record cash.
2. __ Dividends are not included in cash flow statements.
3. __ Income statements reflect current status better than cash flow statements.

Vocabulary

3 Match the words or phrases (1-5) with the definitions (A-E).

1. __ cash flow
2. __ generate
3. __ proceeds
4. __ financing activities
5. __ cumulative

A. receiving money from investors or creditors
B. created by incremental additions
C. the process of money moving into and out of a company
D. to make or create
E. money earned from a sale

4 Fill in the blanks with the correct words or phrases from the word bank.

inflow   stockholder
cash distributions
outflow   dividends

1. The company makes _____ to the owners every month.
2. Every _____ owns a tiny portion of the company.
3. Any time money is spent, it is recorded as a(n) _____.
4. The company pays quarterly _____ to the stockholders.
5. Money received for sales is a(n) _____ of cash.

5 🎧 Listen and read the statement and article again. Why might a cash flow statement and an income statement have a big balance difference?

Listening

6 🎧 Listen to a conversation between a manager and an accountant. Choose the correct answers.

1 What is the dialogue mostly about?
   A money generated from sales
   B accounts receivable payments
   C errors on an income statement
   D contents of cash flow statements

2 The cash flow statement only counts
   A net income.
   B sales amounts.
   C cumulative cash.
   D accounts receivable.

7 🎧 Listen again and complete the conversation.

Manager:	Hi, David. Could I talk to you for a second?
Accountant:	Sure. **1** _____ _____ ?
Manager:	Well, our income statement shows a net income of $200,000.
Accountant:	That **2** _____ about right.
Manager:	But the cash flow statement shows only $100,000 **3** _____ from sales.
Accountant:	Oh, well, the cash flow statement only counts cumulative cash – the **4** _____ cash we spend and receive.
Manager:	So ... Are you **5** _____ me that we haven't received some of the payments on our accounts receivable?
Accountant:	Exactly. But our accounts receivable should **6** _____ _____ for it by next month.

Speaking

8 With a partner, act out the roles below based on Task 7. Then switch roles.

USE LANGUAGE SUCH AS:
Could I talk to you for a second?
The cash flow statement only shows ...
Are you telling me ...?

Student A: You are a manager. Talk to Student B about:
• a cash flow statement
• low/high figures
• what the figures mean

Student B: You are an accountant. Answer Student A's questions.

Writing

9 Use the conversation from Task 8 to complete the email. Make up names for the CPA and Manager.

FROM: _____ CPA _____
TO: _____ , Manager _____

I received your email about the different numbers on the income statement and the cash flow statement. Let me explain why they are different.

21

10 Describing Change

2010 Annual Sales Report

Between January and March, revenue **hovered** around $35,000. In April, the cost of goods went up **slightly**. As a result, we increased prices. This had a negative effect on sales. In fact, revenue **plummeted sharply** to $20,000.

From April to June, revenue **stabilized** and **steadily** increased. In July, sales dropped **dramatically** from $28,000 to just $19,000. This was the result of a new competitor opening up across town.

We **recovered** quickly in September just before the busy season. This was partly due to a sharp **decline** in cost of goods. It allowed us to lower our prices. From October through December, we experienced our usual seasonal increases.

Revenue 2010

rise, increase, go up | fall, decrease, go down | stable, unchanged | fluctuating, unstable | sharp/dramatic increase, skyrocket | sharp/dramatic decrease, plummet

Get Ready!

1 Before you read the passage, talk about these questions.

1. What words describe changing amounts?
2. What are some of the ways to say something increased or decreased?

Reading

2 Read the graph and the company's annual report. Then, mark the following statements as true (T) or false (F).

1. __ Revenue usually increases during a certain season.
2. __ Revenue dropped after a new store opened.
3. __ The company's revenue declined from April to June.

Vocabulary

3 Match the words (1-5) with the definitions (A-E).

1 __ steadily   4 __ slightly
2 __ stabilize   5 __ dramatically
3 __ plummet

A to stop changing
B to drop very far quickly
C without much change; consistently
D with great, rapid change
E to change in a small way

4 Fill in the blanks with the correct words from the word bank.

 BANK

hovered   recovered   declined   sharply

1. The company _____ from its losses.
2. Sales _____ and the company went out of business.
3. Net income had minimal movement; it _____ at a moderate level.
4. Due to a large increase in costs, profits fell _____ .

5 🎧 Listen and read the annual report again. What enabled the company to drop their prices?

Listening

6 🎧 Listen to a conversation between a manager and an accountant. Choose the correct answers.

1. What is the dialogue mostly about?
   A the effects of competition on setting prices
   B reasons why the company must decrease prices
   C the results of the holiday season price increases
   D the causes of changes in sales revenue throughout the year

2. What caused an additional increase in sales revenue?
   A a decrease in prices
   B an increase in advertising
   C an unusually busy holiday season
   D a competitor going out of business

7 🎧 Listen again and complete the conversation.

Accountant: Here's the sales report, Mr. Porter.
Manager: Ah, yes, thank you. Wow. Sales revenue really **1** _____ in April.
Accountant: Yes, it did. I'm **2** _____ _____ why.
Manager: Well, it was **3** _____ a result of our price increases.
Accountant: That **4** _____ _____ . But why did sales increase so much from October to December?
Manager: Well, that's the holiday season.
Accountant: Yes, but I've never seen sales go **5** _____ _____ . What else caused it?
Manager: It's probably **6** _____ _____ Mike's Toy Shop going out of business. They were major competition.

Speaking

8 With a partner, act out the roles below based on Task 7. Then switch roles.

USE LANGUAGE SUCH AS:
Sales revenue really ...
I'm not sure why.
It's probably due to ...

Student A: You are an accountant. Talk to Student B about:
- rising/falling revenue
- causes

Student B: You are a manager. Answer Student A's questions.

Writing

9 Use the graph and the conversation from Task 8 to fill out the sales report. Make up a name for the accountant.

ANNUAL SALES REPORT

Prepared by _____ _____

Between January and March, sales revenue _____
_____
_____

In April, the cost of goods increased _____
As a result, we increased prices _____
sales revenue plummeted _____

In July, sales revenue, although previously stabilized, _____
_____

This was a result of _____
_____

From October through December, _____
_____
_____

23

11 Gleaning Information from Financial Statements

Get Ready!

1 Before you read the passage, talk about these questions.

1. How do accountants use records to determine the health of companies?
2. What are some of the ways they interpret financial records?

Reading

2 Read the email. Then, choose the correct answers.

From: John Simmons, Senior Accountant
To: Becky Johnson, Human Resources; Charles Stanley, Sales; Nicolas Long, Marketing

Good morning! Many employees complain about keeping records. We do keep lots of records, but there's a good reason. We need them to **assess** the health of the company. Here are some ways we **interpret** your records.

Return on Sales
Net Income ÷ Revenue = Return on Sales

Return on Equity
Net Income ÷ Equity = Return on Equity

Year-Over-Year Growth Rate
Profit 2015 ÷ Profit 2014 = Year-Over-Year Growth Rate

These equations and others help us examine **factors** that **eat away at** our profits. Last year we had **thin** profits. Because we had accurate records, we found out that it was due to **uncollectible** receivables.

---

1. What is the passage mainly about?
   - A opportunities for growth
   - B ways to interpret financial records
   - C methods for reducing return on sales
   - D options for increasing return on equity

2. Which equation is NOT presented in the email?
   - A Return on Equity
   - B Return on Sales
   - C Return on receivables
   - D Year-Over-Year Growth

3. What can be inferred about the company's customers?
   - A They keep detailed records.
   - B Some expect a high return on sales.
   - C They interpret financial information.
   - D Some do not pay for their purchases.

Vocabulary

3 Match the words (1-5) with the definitions (A-E).

1. __ assess
2. __ factor
3. __ thin
4. __ return on sales
5. __ return on equity

A not having much substance; small in quantity
B net income in comparison to total revenue
C something that has an influence on something else
D net income in comparison to the value of the company
E to test something

4 Fill in the blanks with the correct words or phrases from the word bank.

WORD BANK

interpret   year-over-year growth rate
uncollectible   eat away at

1. The _____ shows that the company is expanding.
2. The company went out of business. Its debts are _____ .
3. It's the accountant's job to _____ the financial records.
4. Declining sales will definitely _____ profits.

5 🎧 Listen and read the email again. How is the year-over-year growth rate calculated?

Listening

6 🎧 Listen to a conversation between a salesperson and an accountant. Mark the following statements as true (T) or false (F).

1. ___ The woman fills out a sales report monthly.
2. ___ The man thinks paperwork is a waste of time.
3. ___ The woman prefers paperwork over selling.

7 🎧 Listen again and complete the conversation.

Salesperson:	Here's my weekly sales report.
Accountant:	Wonderful. Thank you.
Salesperson:	I'm 1 _____ . Why do we have to keep such 2 _____ records?
Accountant:	Because they help us 3 _____ the company's health. Why do you ask?
Salesperson:	Well, it 4 _____ me down. I'd rather 5 _____ _____ selling than doing paperwork.
Accountant:	I know what you mean. It takes time to 6 _____ _____ . But it's worth it.
Salesperson:	How so?
Accountant:	Accurate records help us see if anything is eating away at our profits.

Speaking

8 With a partner, act out the roles below based on Task 7. Then switch roles.

USE LANGUAGE SUCH AS:

I'm curious. Why do we ... .
Because ... . Why do you ask?
I know what you mean.

Student A: You are a salesperson. Talk to Student B about:
- sales reports
- their purpose
- their uses

Student B: You are an accountant. Answer Student A's questions.

Writing

9 Use the email and the conversation from Task 8 to fill out the financial statement.

FINANCIAL STATEMENT

Profit 2010	11,750
Profit 2011	13,500
Sales revenue	56,500
Net income (profit)	13,500
Owner's equity	41,000

Return on Sales

_____ ÷ _____ = _____

Return on Equity

_____ ÷ _____ = _____

Year-Over-Year Growth Rate

_____ ÷ _____ = _____

12 Overdrafts

Get Ready!

1 Before you read the passage, talk about these questions.

1 What happens if you write a check for more money than you have in your bank account?
2 What are the penalties for overdrawing a bank account?

Reading

2 Read the notice from a bank. Then, choose the correct answers.

1 What is the passage mainly about?
  A a missing check
  B an excessive bank fee
  C an overdrawn bank account
  D an upcoming account statement

2 How can Mr. Johnson compensate for the overdraft?
  A pay the bank $235
  B pay the bank $200
  C request a transfer
  D choose a different bank

3 What can be inferred about overdraft charges?
  A Some of them can be negotiated.
  B There are new charges for every overdraft.
  C They vary according to the overdraft amount.
  D Customer service representatives can block them.

Vocabulary

3 Match the words or phrases (1-5) with the definitions (A-E).

1 ___ overdraft   4 ___ upcoming
2 ___ compensate   5 ___ cash a check
3 ___ transfer

A appearing or arriving in the near future
B to receive money in exchange for a document
C a withdrawal that exceeds an account's balance
D to restore or replace something
E to move something from one place to another

FIRST VENTURE BANK
2437 COMMERCE STREET - NEW YORK, NY 10014

Thomas H. Johnson
Capital Incorporated
10 West 39th Street
Chicago, IL 60610

Dear Mr. Johnson,
Account No. 58756

We regret to **inform** you that you have an **overdraft** of $200.00 on your account. On April 3, 2010, Total Value Office Supply **cashed a check** in the amount of $500.00. Your account balance on that date was $300.00. Your **upcoming** statement includes overdraft **charges** in the amount of $35.00. To avoid further charges, please do not make any additional **withdrawals** or **transfers** until **compensating** for this overdraft. If you have any questions or concerns, please contact us. For your convenience, customer service representatives are available twenty-four hours a day by phone.

4 Fill in the blanks with the correct words from the word bank.

word BANK

charges   withdrawal   inform

1. _____ the manager of the change.
2. Susan needs cash, so she went to her bank and made a(n) _____ .
3. Tom paid a lot of extra _____ because of his overdraft.

5 🎧 Listen and read the notice again. What will show on Capital Incorporated's next statement?

Listening

6 🎧 Listen to a conversation between an accountant and a banker. Mark the following statements as true (T) or false (F).

1. __ The woman's personal account was overdrawn.
2. __ Both accounts now have $500 in them.
3. __ The man refunded the overdraft charges.

7 🎧 Listen again and complete the conversation.

Banker:	First Venture Bank. How may I help you?
Accountant:	Hi. This is Wendy from Capital Incorporated. I just received an 1 _____ _____ from you.
Banker:	I can help you with that. What is your 2 _____ _____ ?
Accountant:	It's 58756. We have a second account with you 3 _____ _____ .
Banker:	Let me see ... Your company's other account has a balance of $1000.00.
Accountant:	Good. Can I 4 _____ $500 into the overdrawn account?
Banker:	5 _____ . Is there anything else I can help you with today?
Accountant:	No, 6 _____ _____ . Thanks.

Speaking

8 With a partner, act out the roles below based on Task 7. Then switch roles.

USE LANGUAGE SUCH AS:
I just received an overdraft notice ...
I can help you with that.
Can I transfer ...?

Student A: You are calling a bank. Talk to Student B about:
- an overdraft
- another account
- paying for the overdraft

Student B: You are a banker. Answer Student A's questions.

Writing

9 Use the notice and the conversation from Task 8 to fill out the email. Make up a name for the accountant.

FROM: _____, Accountant
TO: _____, Manager
RE: an overdraft

Dear _____ ,
I'm writing to inform you of an overdraft and what I did to compensate for it. _____
_____
_____
_____
_____
_____

Cordially,
_____

13 Costs

Why Are Managers Obsessed With Cost?

Setting sales price

Managers set **sales price** by using **markups** or the **cost-plus method**. How? It's simple. Start with the cost of producing something. Then add a certain percentage. This percentage includes the desired profit and fixed expense recovery. But what if a company sells below cost?

markup

Dumping

Sometimes, businesses try to gain an advantage by selling **below cost**. This is called dumping. Many countries have passed laws against dumping. It is a **predatory** pricing practice because companies use it to drive competitors **out of business**. Businesses can only lower their prices down to their costs. Otherwise, someone can **sue** them.

Get Ready!

1 Before you read the passage, talk about these questions.

1. How do companies set prices?
2. How can companies get in trouble for their prices?

Reading

2 Read the magazine article. Then, choose the correct answers.

1. What is the passage mainly about?
   A setting sales prices
   B influencing competitors
   C lowering fixed expenses
   D preventing rising expenses

2. Businesses are only allowed to lower prices if
   A they are dumping.
   B they remain above their costs.
   C they are being sued.
   D their competitors agree.

3. What can be inferred about dumping?
   A It is considered ethical.
   B It is legal in some countries.
   C It involves the markup method.
   D It doesn't account for fixed expenses.

predatory

Vocabulary

3 Match the words or phrases (1-4) with the definitions (A-D).

1 __ sales price   3 __ markup
2 __ dumping   4 __ sue

A an amount added to costs when setting prices
B the amount a business charges for product
C setting a price below costs
D to initiate legal proceedings against someone

4 Fill in the blanks with the correct words or phrases from the word bank.

WORD BANK

below cost   predatory
cost-plus method   out of business

1. Low prices can drive competitors _____ .
2. Dumping is considered a _____ pricing practice.
3. The _____ involves adding a certain percentage.
4. The company is being sued because it was pricing _____ .

5 🎧 Listen and read the article again. What illegal practice do some businesses use and why?

Listening

6 🎧 Listen to a conversation between two accountants. Mark the following statements as true (T) or false (F).

1. __ The woman is surprised by the lawsuit.
2. __ The man often makes purchases from the company.
3. __ The woman thinks the company was acting against the law.

7 🎧 Listen again and complete the conversation.

Accountant 1:	Did you hear about Smithson Technologies?
Accountant 2:	No. Did something **1** _____ _____ them?
Accountant 1:	They're **2** _____ _____ .
Accountant 2:	Really? I hadn't heard that. Why?
Accountant 1:	The lawsuit says they were dumping. It doesn't **3** _____ me. Their prices seemed too low.
Accountant 2:	Personally, I think it's great when a company can offer a **4** _____ product for less money.
Accountant 1:	But if they're selling **5** _____ _____ , it's against the pricing laws.
Accountant 2:	I see **6** _____ _____ . Maybe they were trying to drive their competitors out of business.

Speaking

8 With a partner, act out the roles below based on Task 7. Then switch roles.

USE LANGUAGE SUCH AS:

Did you hear about ...?
They're getting sued.
It doesn't surprise me. Their prices ...

Student A: You are an accountant. Talk to Student B about:
- a lawsuit
- reasons for it
- pricing laws

Student B: You are an accountant. Answer Student A's questions.

Writing

9 Use the conversation from Task 8 to fill out the email. Make up names for the accountant and manager.

FROM: _____, Accountant
TO: _____, Manager
RE: dumping

Dear _____,

As you requested, here is some information about pricing laws. _____
_____
_____
_____

Cordially,
_____

29

14 Taxes

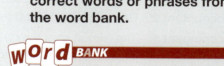

Get Ready!

1 Before you read the passage, talk about these questions.

1. What are some different types of taxes?
2. How do accountants help with taxes?

Reading

2 Read the advertisement from an accounting firm. Then, mark the following statements as true (T) or false (F).

1. __ The firm works with both individuals and corporations.
2. __ The company does not fill out tax forms.
3. __ There is an additional fee for filing with the IRS.

Vocabulary

3 Match the words or phrases (1-5) with the definitions (A-E).

1. __ corporate tax
2. __ property tax
3. __ file
4. __ sales tax
5. __ inheritance tax

A. money that businesses pay to a government
B. money that is paid to a government after a person dies
C. a fee that local governments charge owners of real estate
D. a fee that governments charge when goods are sold
E. to submit documents to a government agency

4 Fill in the blanks with the correct words or phrases from the word bank.

Word BANK
value-added tax   specialize
IRS   excise tax   tax forms

1. In addition to paying taxes, people also have to file _____ .
2. The _____ is the U.S. agency in charge of taxation.
3. Accountants sometimes _____ in a certain type of accounting.
4. _____ is a fee for producing products like fuel and tobacco.
5. _____ is charged at each step in the manufacturing process.

5 🎧 Listen and read the advertisement again. Which area is Calvin Dean and Associates dedicated to?

Listening

6 🎧 Listen to a conversation between an accountant and her client. Choose the correct answers.

1 What is the dialogue mostly about?
   A selling materials
   B increasing sales tax
   C describing new taxes
   D explaining a type of tax

2 Value-added tax
   A adds value to products.
   B was replaced by sales tax.
   C has not been adopted in the USA.
   D is applied when final products are sold.

7 🎧 Listen again and complete the conversation.

Accountant:	How are you today, Mr. Jackson?
Client:	I'm good. Could you **1** _____ something for me?
Accountant:	Sure. What is it?
Client:	Well, I **2** _____ _____ _____ what value-added tax is.
Accountant:	It's like sales tax. When a company sells **3** _____ or parts to another, they pay a tax.
Client:	So, does that **4** _____ _____ my company?
Accountant:	No. You only **5** _____ _____ in the United States, which hasn't adopted a value-added tax yet.
Client:	Oh, I see. So that's not something I need **6** _____ _____ _____.

Speaking

8 With a partner, act out the roles below based on Task 7. Then switch roles.

USE LANGUAGE SUCH AS:
Could you clarify something for me?
I have no idea what ... is.
It's ...

Student A: You are talking to an accountant. Talk to Student B about:
• value-added tax
• how it works
• if it applies to you

Student B: You are an accountant. Answer Student A's questions.

Writing

9 Use the conversation from Task 8 to fill out the email. Make up a name for the accountant.

FROM: Donald Benton, Manager
RE: value-added tax

What is value-added tax? Does it apply to us?

DB

[reply]

_____, Accountant
FROM: _____

Mr. Benton,

Value-added tax is _____
_____
_____
_____

Cordially,
_____

31

15 Depreciation

straight-line depreciation

accelerated depreciation

MEMORANDUM

From: Bill Anderson
To: All Staff

Good morning team! I want to offer the best service to our clients. To do that, we need to review **depreciation**. There are two **depreciation methods**. We must consider each client's needs when deciding which to use.

Straight-line depreciation evenly decreases the value of a **depreciable asset** through the entire **recovery period**.

Accelerated depreciation accounts for more **wear and tear** during the first years of a **tangible asset**'s use.

Each **depreciation schedule** is useful. Both end with the same **salvage value**. Depreciate assets like cars, that go through a lot of wear and tear with the accelerated method. Depreciate assets, like computers, that suffer **obsolescence** with the straight-line method.

Get Ready!

1 Before you read the passage, talk about these questions.

1 What are some assets that lose value quickly?
2 What are some assets that are eventually worth nothing?

Reading

2 Read the memo from a partner in an accounting firm. Then, choose the correct answers.

1 What is the passage mainly about?
   A avoiding obsolescence
   B decreasing wear and tear
   C buying salvaged property
   D accounting for changing value

2 The straight-line method is used to depreciate assets
   A that suffer obsolescence.
   B during their first few years.
   C that experience wear and tear.
   D with unpredictable salvage value.

3 Accelerated depreciation
   A prevents obsolescence.
   B decreases value evenly.
   C expands the recovery period.
   D accounts for damage from use.

Vocabulary

3 Match the words or phrases (1-6) with the definitions (A-F).

1 __ depreciation
2 __ recovery period
3 __ salvage value
4 __ tangible asset
5 __ depreciation method
6 __ wear and tear

A a physical object that holds value
B the process by which assets lose their value
C what an asset is worth after losing value
D the time in which depreciation is accounted for
E the way in which an asset's loss of value is recorded
F damage that occurs through normal use

4 Fill in the blanks with the correct words or phrases from the word bank.

Word BANK

straight-line depreciation
accelerated depreciation   depreciable assets
obsolescence   depreciation schedule

1 Use _____ with the car; it loses value quickly in the first years.
2 Use _____ to reduce value at a steady rate.
3 How an asset loses value determines what _____ should be used.
4 Most objects that hold value, except real estate, are _____.
5 Electronic assets like computers and cell phones suffer _____.

5 🎧 Listen and read the memo again. What is meant by the term depreciation?

Listening

6 🎧 Listen to a conversation between an accountant and her client. Mark the following statements as true (T) or false (F).

1 __ The man recently sold an air conditioner.
2 __ The woman recommends straight-line depreciation.
3 __ Straight-line depreciation is the most complicated method.

7 🎧 Listen again and complete the conversation.

Accountant:	Hello, Tony. What can I do for you?
Client:	Well, I **1** _____ _____ a new air conditioner. Is it an expense or a depreciable asset?
Accountant:	An air conditioner? That's a depreciable asset.
Client:	OK. So, I need to **2** _____ _____ depreciation to keep my books **3** _____.
Accountant:	Right. Which depreciation schedule do you want to use?
Client:	I don't know. I want something simple and easy.
Accountant:	**4** _____ _____ using the straight-line method? That's the **5** _____.
Client:	That **6** _____ _____ to me.

Speaking

8 With a partner, act out the roles below based on Task 7. Then switch roles.

USE LANGUAGE SUCH AS:

I bought a ... Is it an expense or ...?
Which depreciation schedule do you ...?
How about using the ...?

Student A: You are calling an accountant. Talk to Student B about:
- a purchase
- depreciation schedules
- which to use

Student B: You are an accountant. Answer Student A's questions.

Writing

9 Use the memo and the conversation from Task 8 to fill out the letter to a client. Make up names for the client and accountant.

Dear _____,

I received your request for information about depreciation. Here are some details about depreciation and the different depreciation schedules that you can use.

_____
_____
_____

Cordially,

_____, CPA

Glossary

accelerated depreciation [N-UNCOUNT-U15] **Accelerated depreciation** is a depreciation schedule in which higher amounts of value are deducted for the first years of the recovery period than for later years.

accounting software [N-UNCOUNT-U5] **Accounting software** is a computer program that records and organizes financial information.

accounts payable [N-PL-U8] **Accounts payable** are the recorded amounts of purchases for which a company has not yet made payment.

accounts receivable [N-PL-U8] **Accounts receivable** are the recorded amounts of sales for which a company has not yet received payment.

add [V-T-U2] To **add** numbers is to combine them.

adjusted trial balance [N-COUNT-U5] An **adjusted trial balance** is a listing of account balances after corrections have been made.

and [CONJ-U2] **and** shows that two things are meant to be put together.

assess [V-T-U11] To **assess** is to test or evaluate something.

asset [N-COUNT-U8] An **asset** is something of value that a company owns.

back-office [N-COUNT-U1] The **back-office** is office space containing a business's accounting, IT, human resources, and other administrative departments.

balance sheet [N-COUNT-U8] A **balance sheet** is a document that shows a company's assets, liabilities, and equity at a certain point in time.

binder [N-COUNT-U3] A **binder** is a notebook that holds papers with rings or clips.

bookkeeper [N-COUNT-U1] A **bookkeeper** is an accountant who records transactions.

broad-scale uniformity [N-UNCOUNT-U6] **Broad-scale uniformity** means that a large number of people or organizations function in an identical manner.

budget analyst [N-COUNT-U1] A **budget analyst** is an accountant who manages a company's financial plans.

bulletin board [N-COUNT-U3] A **bulletin board** is a wall panel that people post messages on.

calculator [N-COUNT-U4] A **calculator** is a hand-held device that performs mathematical operations.

cash a check [PHR-U12] To **cash a check** is to exchange a check for money.

cash distribution [N-COUNT-U9] A **cash distribution** is a periodic payment made to the owner(s) of a company.

cash flow [N-UNCOUNT-U9] **Cash flow** is the process of money moving into and out of a company.

CD/DVD drive [N-COUNT-U4] A **CD/DVD** drive is an optical disc drive that reads and writes data on CDs and DVDs.

charge [N-COUNT-U12] A **charge** is a fee associated with an inappropriate transaction.

client [N-COUNT-U1] A **client** is a customer or person for whom services are provided.

compensate [V-T-U12] To **compensate** for something is to make amends for it.

consistent [ADJ-U6] If something is **consistent**, it adheres to a certain standard without varying.

copier [N-COUNT-U4] A **copier** is a machine that produces duplicates of paper documents.

corporate tax [N-COUNT-U14] A **corporate tax** is a fee that a government charges businesses.

cost-plus method [N-UNCOUNT-U13] The **cost-plus method** is the act of adding a certain percentage to costs when setting sales prices.

CPA [N-COUNT-U1] **CPA** stands for Certified Public Accountant. It is a position licensed by the government.

credit card statement [N-COUNT-U5] A **credit card statement** is a document showing all purchases and payments associated with a credit card.

cubicle divider [N-COUNT-U3] A **cubicle divider** is a temporary structure that divides office space.

cumulative [ADJ-U9] **Cumulative** means put together by a series of additions.

debt [N-COUNT-U8] **Debt** is money that has been borrowed, usually from a bank.

decline [V-I-U10] To **decline** is to decrease.

depreciable asset [N-COUNT-U15] A **depreciable asset** is any piece of physical property that loses value over time.

depreciation [N-NOCOUNT-U15] **Depreciation** is the process by which assets lose value over time.

depreciation method [N-COUNT-U15] A **depreciation method** is an accounting technique that records reductions in value.

depreciation schedule [N-COUNT-U15] A **depreciation schedule** is a long-term plan for how and when depreciation will occur.

desk lamp [N-COUNT-U3] A **desk lamp** is a device that provides light for a desk.

desktop computer [N-COUNT-U4] A **desktop computer** is a stationary computer.

disclosure [N-COUNT-U6] **Disclosure** is a release of information.

divided by [PREP-U2] **Divided by** means that a number is meant to be broken into equal units of a certain quantity.

dividend [N-COUNT-U9] A **dividend** is a portion of profits given to a stockholder based on what percentage of the company he or she owns.

dramatically [ADV-U10] To do something **dramatically** means to do it in an intense or extreme way.

drive competitors out of business [V-PHRASE-U13] To **drive competitors out of business** is to draw so many customers away from competitors' stores that they don't make enough money to stay in business.

dry eraser [N-COUNT-U3] A **dry eraser** is a block of soft material used to erase the words or diagrams from a white board.

dumping [N-UNCOUNT-U13] **Dumping** is the act of selling goods below cost.

eat away at [V-T-U11] To **eat away at** something is to gradually remove parts of it or otherwise reduce it.

end-of-period procedure [N-COUNT-U5] An **end-of-period procedure** is a task that must be done at the end of an accounting period before opening books for a new period.

equals [V-T-U2] **Equals** means that two things are the same.

excise tax [N-COUNT-U14] An **excise tax** is a fee for producing certain non-essential products like tobacco and fuel.

Glossary

factor [N-COUNT-U11] A **factor** is anything that influences something else.

FASB [N-COUNT-U6] **FASB** stands for Financial Accounting Standards Board, which establishes GAAP.

fax machine [N-COUNT-U4] A **fax machine** is a device that encodes and sends paper documents over phone lines.

file [V-T-U14] To **file** something is to turn it in to the agency that requires it.

file cabinet [N-COUNT-U3] A **file cabinet** is a set of drawers that people store records in.

file clerk [N-COUNT-U1] A **file clerk** is an employee who maintains files and records.

financing activity [N-COUNT-U9] **Financing activities** are things that companies do to increase the amount of cash they have (e.g., taking out a loan, selling portions of the company to stockholders).

firm [N-COUNT-U1] A **firm** is a business that provides professional services like legal counsel, accounting, design, etc.

fiscal year [N-COUNT-U5] A **fiscal year** is the period used by organizations to prepare annual financial statements.

fixed asset [N-COUNT-U8] A **fixed asset** is any piece of property that is not easily converted to cash (e.g., a building).

flash drive [N-COUNT-U4] A **flash drive** is a data storage device using a memory chip.

GAAP [N-COUNT-U6] **GAAP** stands for Generally Accepted Accounting Principles. These principles are the primary accounting standards in the US.

general and administrative costs [N-COUNT-U7] **General and administrative costs** are the amounts of money that must be spent to organize and run a company.

generate [V-T-U9] To **generate** something is to create it.

governing body [N-COUNT-U6] A **governing body** is a regulatory or advisory organization that makes rules or suggestions.

gross margin [N-COUNT-U7] The **gross margin** is the amount of money left when cost of goods sold is subtracted from sales revenue.

hover [V-I-U10] To **hover** means to stay near a particular point.

IASB [N-COUNT-U6] **IASB** stands for International Accounting Standards Board, which establishes accounting standards in Europe.

income statement [N-COUNT-U7] An **income statement** is a document that shows how much money an organization gained or lost in a certain period of time.

inflow [N-UNCOUNT-U9] **Inflow** is cash coming into a company.

inform [V-T-U12] To **inform** someone about something is to tell him or her about it.

inheritance tax [N-COUNT-U14] An **inheritance tax** is a requirement that people give a certain portion of a deceased person's assets to the government.

internal auditor [N-COUNT-U1] An **internal auditor** is an employee hired by a company to monitor its financial activities.

interpret [V-T-U11] To **interpret** is to determine the appropriate meaning of something.

inventory [N-UNCOUNT-U8] **Inventory** is the value of products that a company has bought and intends to sell for profit.

IRS [N-UNCOUNT-U14] The **IRS** (Internal Revenue Service) is the taxation agency in the United States

is [V-U2] **Is** shows that two things are the same.

landline phone [N-COUNT-U4] A **landline phone** is a device used to talk to people across great distances using cables.

laptop computer [N-COUNT-U4] A **laptop computer** is a portable computer.

less [PREP-U2] **Less** means that one quantity is meant to be taken away from another.

liability [N-COUNT-U8] A **liability** is any amount of money that a company owes.

markup [N-COUNT-U13] A **markup** is a certain amount of money that companies add to their costs when setting sales prices.

minus [PREP-U2] **Minus** means that one quantity is meant to be taken away from another.

mobile phone [N-COUNT-U4] A **mobile phone** is a device used to talk to people across great distances using radio waves.

multiplied by [PREP-U2] **Multiplied by** means that a number is meant to be added to itself a certain number of times.

net income [N-COUNT-U7] **Net income** is the amount of money that remains after all expenses have been deducted from sales revenue.

note pad [N-COUNT-U3] A **note pad** is a book of blank paper for writing on.

obsolescence [N-UNCOUNT-U15] **Obsolescence** is a state in which an item is no longer useful because it has been replaced by more advanced alternatives.

operating margin [N-COUNT-U7] The **operating margin** is the amount of money left when general and administrative costs are subtracted from the gross margin.

outflow [N-UNCOUNT-U9] **Outflow** is cash moving out of a company.

over [PREP-U2] **Over** means that a number is meant to be divided by another number.

overdraft [N-COUNT-U12] An **overdraft** is a transaction conducted without sufficient funds.

owner's equity [N-UNCOUNT-U8] **Owner's equity** is the total monetary value of a company.

P & L [N-COUNT-U7] A **P & L** is a profit and loss statement. It shows how much money an organization gained or lost in a certain period of time.

paper clip [N-COUNT-U3] A **paper clip** is a small device that holds sheets of paper together.

payroll [N-UNCOUNT-U5] **Payroll** is a list of employees and their salaries or wages.

payroll master file [N-COUNT-U5] A **payroll master file** is a file containing all of a company's payroll information.

plummet [V-I-U10] To **plummet** is to decrease rapidly.

plus [PREP-U2] **Plus** means that two quantities are meant to be combined.

predatory pricing practice [N-COUNT-U13] A **predatory pricing practice** is an activity designed to deliberately drive competitors out of business.

principles-based approach [N-COUNT-U6] A **principles-based approach** is a method of setting accounting standards based on guiding principles.

Glossary

printer [N-COUNT-U4] A **printer** is a machine that transfers documents from computer files to paper.

proceeds [N-UNCOUNT-U9] **Proceeds** are monies received from sales.

property tax [N-COUNT-U14] A **property tax** is a fee that local governments charge for owning real estate.

purchase invoice [N-COUNT-U5] A **purchase invoice** is a document requesting that payment be made for a purchase.

recover [V-I-U10] To **recover** is to achieve a normal level after a decrease.

recovery period [N-COUNT-U15] A **recovery period** is the length of time during which an asset is depreciated.

return on equity [N-UNCOUNT-U11] **Return on equity** is a comparison of net income to owner's equity.

return on sales [N-UNCOUNT-U11] **Return on sales** is a comparison of net income to sales revenue.

rules-based approach [N-COUNT-U6] A **rules-based approach** is a method of setting accounting standards based on non-negotiable rules.

sales price [N-COUNT-U13] A **sales price** is the amount of money that someone requires in exchange for an item.

sales revenue [N-COUNT-U7] **Sales revenue** is the amount of money that is received from selling goods or services.

sales tax [N-COUNT-U14] A **sales tax** is a fee that the government charges for selling a product or service.

salvage value [N-COUNT-U15] **Salvage value** is what an asset is worth after being depreciated across its recovery period.

sell below cost [V-PHRASE-U13] To **sell below cost** is to the sell something for less money than it took to purchase, manufacture or produce it.

selling [N-UNCOUNT-U7] **Selling** is the act of exchanging goods or services for money.

sharply [ADV-U10] To do something **sharply** is to do it rapidly.

slightly [ADV-U10] To do something **slightly** means to do it to a small degree.

source document [N-COUNT-U5] A **source document** is one of the various types of records of financial transactions.

specialize [V-T-U14] To **specialize** in something is to acquire a high level of knowledge and experience with it.

stabilize [V-I-U10] To **stabilize** is to achieve and maintain a steady level.

stapler [N-COUNT-U3] A **stapler** is a device that fastens together sheets of paper by piercing them with staples.

steadily [ADV-U10] To do something **steadily** means to do it at a constant, stable rate.

stockholder [N-COUNT-U9] A **stockholder** is a person who has purchased a percentage of ownership of a company.

straight-line depreciation [N-UNCOUNT-U15] **Straight-line depreciation** is a depreciation schedule in which an asset's value is deducted at a steady rate.

subtract [V-T-U2] To **subtract** a number is to remove that quantity from another number.

sue [V-T-U13] To **sue** someone is to initiate legal proceedings against them.

sum [N-COUNT-U8] A **sum** is the result of adding two or more numbers.

tangible asset [N-COUNT-U15] A **tangible asset** is any piece of physical property that bears value.

tax [N-COUNT-U7] **Tax** is money that individuals and businesses are required to pay to a government.

tax accountant [N-COUNT-U1] A **tax accountant** is an accountant who specializes in tax regulations.

tax form [N-COUNT-U14] A **tax form** is a document that people and corporations are required to turn in to the government's taxation agency.

thin [ADJ-U11] If something is **thin**, it does not have much substance.

time card [N-COUNT-U5] A **time card** is a card or document showing the hours that an employee worked.

times [PREP-U2] **Times** means that numbers are meant to be multiplied.

trainee [N-COUNT-U1] A **trainee** is an employee who is learning a new job.

transaction [N-COUNT-U5] A **transaction** is an event in which money is exchanged for goods or services.

transfer [N-COUNT-U12] A **transfer** is the act of moving money from one account to another.

uncollectible [ADJ-U11] If something is **uncollectible**, it cannot be found, received, or taken.

upcoming [ADJ-U12] If something is **upcoming**, it will soon arrive or appear.

value-added tax [N-COUNT-U14] **Value-added tax** consists of fees that are charged every time materials are transferred from one company to another during the manufacturing process.

wear and tear [N-UNCOUNT-U15] **Wear and tear** is damage that occurs to an item while it is being used.

whiteboard [N-COUNT-U3] A **whiteboard** is a writing surface that things can be erased from.

withdrawal [N-COUNT-U12] A **withdrawal** is the act of removing money from an account.

year-over-year growth rate [N-COUNT-U11] The **year-over-year growth rate** is a comparison of one year's profits to another year's profits.

Accounting

Book 2

John Taylor
Stephen Peltier - C.P.A., M.S.

Scope and Sequence

Unit	Topic	Reading context	Vocabulary	Function
1	The Back Office	Journal Article	back office, cash collections, checking account, gross earnings, gross wages, pay stub, procurement, purchase order, salary, total wages	Stating a preference
2	Guiding Principles of Accounting	Textbook	business entity, conservatism, corporation, full disclosure, most-likely scenario, objectivity, optimistic, partnership, relevance, sole proprietorship, unbiased	Talking about opinions
3	Controllers	Job Listing	accounting system, attention to detail, background check, CFO, controller, drug screening, external financial report, integrity, internal financial report, up to date	Asking about priorities
4	Cash and Liquidity	Journal Article	buy out, excessive, expenditures, insufficient, liquidity, receipt, safety reserve, unproductive, zero cash balance	Stating an opinion
5	Intangible Assets	Magazine Article	amortization, competitive intangible, copyright, goodwill, intangible assets, legal intangibles, patent rights, trade secrets, trademark	Requesting explantation
6	Presenting a P & L Statement	Memo	EBIT, fixed expenses, margin per unit, operating earnings, profit center, retailer, sales volume, total margin, variable expenses, wholesaler	Describing uncertainty
7	Internal Controls Against Mistakes and Theft	Journal Article	accounting controls, deceit, embezzlement, falsification, forgery, fraud, hold accountable, kick-back, misappropriation, pilfering, shoplift	Making plans
8	Accrual Basis Accounting – Non-cash Accounts	Textbook	accounts payable, accounts receivable, accrual basis accounting, advance payment, allocate, increment, on credit, paid for ahead of time, prepaid expense account	Asking for clarification
9	Unpaid Expenses	Textbook	accrual, accrued expenses payable, bill, bonus, carry over, income tax payable, load period, via	Asking about methods
10	Leverage – Good or Bad	Magazine Article	collateral, default, desirable terms, interest rate, leverage, origination fee, pay off, senior claim, take out, tax deductible	Giving a negative reaction
11	Variable Expenses	Report	campaign, charitable, discontinue, employee benefits, level off, profit sharing plan, repair, spike, temporary	Listing possible causes
12	End-of-Period Procedures	Email	abnormally, adjusting entries, audit trail, catch my attention, flow of transactions, out of the ordinary, red flag, stiff, sweep	Talking about completion
13	Accounting Software	Advertisement	data mining, ease of use, functionality, "garbage in, garbage out", remote access, security, up and running, user license, user-friendly	Discussing function
14	Reporting Extraordinary Gains and Losses	Journal Article	damages, discontinuity, downsizing, extraordinary, impaired, layoff, lawsuit, restructuring, severance package	Describing limits
15	Is Profit Ethical?	Article	condemn, criticize, environmentally friendly, ethical, exploit, immoral, low road, make a killing, unethical	Describing frequency

Table of Contents

Unit 1 – The Back Office 4

Unit 2 – Guiding Principles of Accounting 6

Unit 3 – Controllers 8

Unit 4 – Cash and Liquidity 10

Unit 5 – Intangible Assets 12

Unit 6 – Presenting a P & L Statement 14

Unit 7 – Internal Controls Against Mistakes and Theft 16

Unit 8 – Accrual Basis Accounting — Non-cash Accounts ... 18

Unit 9 – Unpaid Expenses 20

Unit 10 – Leverage — Good or Bad? 22

Unit 11 – Variable Expenses 24

Unit 12 – End-of-Period Procedures 26

Unit 13 – Accounting Software 28

Unit 14 – Reporting Extraordinary Gains and Losses 30

Unit 15 – Is Profit Ethical? 32

Glossary 34

1 The Back Office

Get ready!

1 Before you read the passage, talk about these questions.

1. What jobs get done in the back office?
2. What are some common accounting tasks?

Reading

2 Read the article in a business journal. Then, choose the correct answers.

1. What is the passage mainly about?
   A periodic cash disbursements
   B informative financial reports
   C routine accounting procedures
   D common back office maintenance

2. _____ show year-to-date earnings and taxes.
   A Pay stubs
   B Purchase orders
   C Cash collections
   D Checking accounts

3. Who does NOT work in the back office?
   A clerks   C accountants
   B bookkeepers   D receptionists

Business and Finance Weekly – Oct. 15

WHAT'S GOING ON IN THE BACK OFFICE?
by Charles Thompson

The Back Office – Accounting
For many people, the back office is a mystery. Data goes in, and informative financial reports come out. But mysterious as it seems, the back office is vital to any business.

What happens in the back office?
The back office is home to clerks, bookkeepers, and accountants. Here is a list of some of the most important accounting tasks:

Payroll
Accountants calculate **salaries** and **total wages** for every employee. These are called **gross earnings** or **gross wages**. The accountants also prepare **pay stubs** for each pay period showing the employees their year-to-date earnings and taxes.

Cash collections
Accountants record cash that the company receives and manage the company's **checking accounts**.

Cash disbursements
Payroll checks are not the only checks that accountants write. They also handle all other cash disbursements.

Procurement
Accountants keep track of a company's inventory. They record all **purchase orders** and make sure they have been filled. •••

Vocabulary

3 Match the words or phrases (1-4) with the definitions (A-D).

1 __ salary   3 __ purchase order
2 __ procurement   4 __ pay stub

A a fixed annual amount of pay
B the act of gathering supplies or inventory
C a document showing an employee's pay and taxes
D a document showing what someone wants to buy

4 Read the sentence pairs. Choose which word or phrase fits each blank.

1 gross wages / procurement
   A To find _____ multiply hours by rate of pay.
   B Have the _____ people check for shipment errors.

2 gross earnings / cash collections
   A The manager's salary before taxes is called _____ .
   B Payments should be directed to the _____ accountant.

3 checking account / total wages
   A _____ are the sum of an employee's hourly pay.
   B Employees are paid from the company's _____ .

5 🎧 Listen and read the article again. What tasks do payroll accountants carry out?

Listening

6 🎧 Listen to a conversation between two accountants. Mark the following statements as true (T) or false (F).

1 __ The company's back office is divided into departments.
2 __ The man wants to work in payroll.
3 __ New employees work in all departments.

7 🎧 Listen again and complete the conversation.

Accountant 2:	Hi, Jason! **1** _____ _____ . Let me show you around.
Accountant 1:	Great. I'm really excited to be here.
Accountant 2:	Well, we're happy **2** _____ _____ _____ . Now, our back office is divided into different **3** _____ _____ .
Accountant 1:	OK. Which one do you work in?
Accountant 2:	Well, I **4** _____ _____ in payroll, but I **5** _____ _____ the other departments.
Accountant 1:	I would love to work in payroll. That was **6** _____ _____ accounting task in school.
Accountant 2:	Well that's possible. We like to place people where they're comfortable.
Accountant 1:	Where do new hires usually start?
Accountant 2:	Well, actually, we train them in all departments.

Speaking

8 With a partner, act out the roles below based on Task 7. Then switch roles.

> **USE LANGUAGE SUCH AS:**
> *Welcome aboard.*
> *I would love to work ...*
> *I usually ... but I sometimes ...*

Student A: It's your first day as an accountant. Talk to Student B about:
• the departments
• your favorite task
• training

Student B: You are a senior accountant. Answer Student A's questions.

Writing

9 Use the conversation from Task 8 to complete the welcome letter.

To Our New Employee

Welcome!

We want to take this opportunity to tell you about your new job.

The Back Office
_____
_____

The Accounting Departments
_____
_____

Our Training Procedures
_____
_____

2 Guiding Principles of Accounting

Get ready!

1 Before you read the passage, talk about these questions.

1. What are some ways that all accountants are the same?
2. What are some principles that every accountant follows?

Reading

2 Read the textbook passage. Then, choose the correct answers.

Fundamental Principles of Accounting

Accountants oversee and record the exchange of money. These talented professionals work in every sector of society. Businesses, governments, and individuals depend on them. And all accountants are guided by the same principles.

Business Entity – Every business is a distinct entity. It is important that its records be kept separate from its owner's records. This is true of any type of business: **partnerships**, **sole proprietorships,** or **corporations**.

Conservatism – Accountants use conservative methods. They account for the **most-likely scenario** rather than the most **optimistic** scenario.

Objectivity – Accountants only use verifiable numbers. They should not allow their feelings or opinions to influence their records. All records must be accurate and **unbiased**.

Relevance – Accountants prepare financial records that are useful to business managers.

Full Disclosure – Accounting records include all available information. Nothing is withheld or hidden.

1. What is the passage mainly about?
   A how to verify objectivity
   B ideas that guide accountants
   C when principles must be changed
   D how to predict the most-likely scenario

2. Relevance means that
   A a sole proprietorship is unbiased.
   B business records must be practical.
   C optimistic scenarios are not hidden.
   D managers should include all information.

3. Objectivity means
   A separating personal records.
   B using only verifiable numbers.
   C following feelings and opinions.
   D accounting for optimistic scenarios.

Vocabulary

3 Match the words or phrases (1-6) with the definitions (A-F).

1. __ unbiased
2. __ relevance
3. __ corporation
4. __ sole proprietorship
5. __ most-likely scenario
6. __ full disclosure

A handling information fairly without prejudice
B the situation which has the greatest chance of happening
C a business owned by one person
D the release of all information
E a business that is legally recognized as a single unit
F the state of being significant

partnership

unbiased

6

4 Fill in the blanks with the correct words or phrases from the word bank.

Word BANK

business entity   partnership
conservatism   optimistic   objectivity

1 Though the economy is bad, Linda is _____ about the future.
2 Every company, no matter what type, is a separate _____.
3 _____ is a company owned by just a few people.
4 Reporting most-likely scenarios is key to the principle of _____.
5 _____ means not letting feelings and opinions get in the way.

5 🎧 Listen and read the textbook passage again. Which principle is synonymous with openness and honesty?

Listening

6 🎧 Listen to a conversation between a radio show host and an accountant. Mark the following statements as true (T) or false (F).

1 ___ There are problems with objectivity at Infinite Time.
2 ___ The man likes Infinite Time watches.
3 ___ The man works for Infinite Time.

7 🎧 Listen again and complete the conversation.

Interviewer:	So, Todd, let's talk about a guiding principle of accounting: Objectivity.
Accountant:	OK. Well, objectivity means that accountants must be **1** _____.
Interviewer:	Uh-huh. What do you mean by that?
Accountant:	Um, let's say I work for a company. How about Infinite Time?
Interviewer:	Infinite Time. That's the **2** _____ _____ company, right?
Accountant:	That's right, they ...
Interviewer:	You know – **3** _____ _____ _____ – I'm wearing an Infinite Time watch.
Accountant:	I see that. It's very nice. Now, I **4** _____ _____ my opinions about Infinite Time to **5** _____ _____ I keep their records.
Interviewer:	Hmm ... like if you said the company is **6** _____ _____ _____ it is because you like their watches?
Accountant:	Exactly. That would be my opinion. But it **7** _____ _____ _____.

Speaking

8 With a partner, act out the roles below based on Task 7. Then switch roles.

USE LANGUAGE SUCH AS:
Let's say I work for ...
... sorry to interrupt ...
I can't allow my opinions about ...

Student A: You're interviewing an accountant. Talk to Student B about:
- objectivity
- what it is
- examples

Student B: You are an accountant. Answer Student A's questions.

Writing

9 Use the textbook passage and the conversation from Task 8 to complete the email. Make up names for the company, accountant, manager and the CPA.

FROM: _____, Accountant Manager

TO: _____, CPA

Next month you will be reviewing some records from ____ Inc. I know that you have worked with that company in the past. I just wanted to remind you to maintain objectivity. _____
_____
_____
_____

Sincerely,
_____

3 Controllers

attention to detail

controller

10 Professionals Monthly – MAY

Wanted: CONTROLLER

The accounting firm of West, Kennedy, and Wilson is seeking a well-qualified **controller**. This position is available immediately.
Requirements:
- A bachelor's or master's degree in Accounting
- Must be a Certified Public Accountant (CPA)
- At least seven years' experience with **accounting systems**
- Management experience is preferred, but not necessary
- Willingness to submit to a **background check** and **drug screening**
- Honesty
- **Integrity**
- **Attention to detail**
- Willingness to travel
- Willingness to work some nights and weekends, as needed

Responsibilities include:
- Ensuring that financial records are kept **up to date**
- Preparing and distributing all final **internal** and **external financial reports**
- Reporting directly to the **Chief Financial Officer (CFO)**
- Oversight and quality assurance of all bookkeeping activities
- Training of new hires and development of standardized training materials

Please submit a resume to the Human Resources Department.

Get ready!

1 Before you read the passage, talk about these questions.

1. What does a controller do?
2. What are the qualifications of a controller?

Reading

2 Read the job advertisement. Then, mark the following statements as true (T) or false (F).

1. __ Applicants must have a college degree.
2. __ The person who gets the job will work some weekends.
3. __ The person who gets the job will teach other employees.

Vocabulary

3 Match the words or phrases (1-5) with the definitions (A-E).

1. __ controller
2. __ integrity
3. __ up to date
4. __ accounting system
5. __ internal financial records

A containing all information as of today
B a uniform set of methods and procedures
C documents that are used by members of an organization
D adhering to morals and professional principles
E a person who oversees a company's financial matters

4 Fill in the blanks with the correct words or phrases: *background check, chief financial officer, drug screening, external financial records, attention to detail.*

1 Todd never used illegal substances, so he easily passed the _____ .

2 Perform a _____ on all employees to see if they have a criminal record.

3 _____ are documents prepared for people outside the company.

4 As the _____ , Henry oversees all accounting activities.

5 Carol has great _____ , and easily finds errors.

5 🎧 Listen and read the job advertisement again. What personal qualities are the employers looking for in a controller?

Listening

6 🎧 Listen to a conversation between a human resources employee and an applicant. Choose the correct answers.

1 What is the dialogue mostly about?
 A interviewing for a job
 B creating a job advertisement
 C designing an accounting system
 D reviewing a new hire's performance

2 The man left his previous job because he
 A lacked honesty and integrity.
 B didn't like the job enough to stay.
 C went to school for a master's degree.
 D couldn't design an accounting system.

7 🎧 Listen again and complete the conversation.

Employee: I have your resume. It says you were a controller for four years
Applicant: I was – at Benjamin Landon and associates.
Employee: And how did you like it?
Applicant: It was a good job. I left to go back to school and get a master's degree.
Employee: I see. So, tell me, what do you think are **1** _____ _____ ?
Applicant: Honesty and integrity. I take my work seriously and **2** _____ _____ _____ from others.
Employee: OK. And what are your **3** _____ _____ ?
Applicant: Um, I haven't designed a **4** _____ _____ _____ yet.
Employee: You didn't do that **5** _____ _____ _____ controller job?
Applicant: No. They had a system in place that they really liked, so I **6** _____ _____ _____ .

Speaking

8 With a partner, act out the roles below based on Task 7. Then switch roles.

USE LANGUAGE SUCH AS:
What do you think are your strengths?
What are your major weaknesses?
I haven't ...

Student A: You're interviewing a job applicant. Talk to Student B about:
• past experience   • strengths   • weaknesses

Student B: You are a job applicant. Answer Student A's questions.

Writing

9 Use the conversation from Task 8 to complete the interviewer's notes. Make up a name for the applicant.

Notes
Applicant's name: _____
Work experience: _____
Education: _____
Strengths/Weaknesses: _____

4 Cash and Liquidity

Money Management – April Edition – page 37

How Liquid is Your Company?

by Sarah Jacobs

Liquidity is a vital factor of your business's health. But what is liquidity? Liquidity refers to your company's ability to meet its obligations without selling assets. The least liquid assets are things like buildings and brand names. These assets take time to be converted to cash.

It is important to maintain a certain level of liquidity. **Excessive** cash balances are **unproductive**. But **insufficient** cash balances are dangerous.

Every day, your business has cash **receipts** and **expenditures**. It is a bad idea to trust that your daily receipts are enough to cover your expenditures. You can't get by with a **zero cash balance**. Instead, maintain a **safety reserve** of cash. The best way to do this is to keep a cash account. This allows you to pay unexpected expenditures. It also sets you up for opportunities like investments or **buying out** competitors. ...

zero cash balance

Get ready!

1 Before you read the passage, talk about these questions.

1. What does 'liquid' mean?
2. What are the most liquid assets?

Reading

2 Read the article from an accounting journal. Then, mark the following statements as true (T) or false (F).

1. ___ Brand names are highly liquid assets.
2. ___ Insufficient cash leads to unexpected expenditures.
3. ___ The author suggests having a safety reserve of cash.

Vocabulary

3 Match the words or phrases (1-5) with the definitions (A-E).

1. ___ liquidity
2. ___ insufficient
3. ___ receipts
4. ___ excessive
5. ___ buy out

A an amount beyond what is needed
B an asset's ability to be converted to cash
C an amount that is less that what is needed
D to purchase a company
E things that are received

4 Fill in the blanks with the correct words or phrases:
expenditures, zero cash balance, unproductive, safety reserve.

1 Make sure there is enough cash to cover _____ .
2 Walter has been putting extra money into a _____ .
3 The company couldn't pay its bill because it had a _____ .
4 Keeping too much money is a cash account is _____ .

5 🎧 Listen and read the article again. Why are cash accounts useful?

Listening

6 🎧 Listen to a conversation between two accountants. Choose the correct answers.

1 What is the dialogue mostly about?
   A how to generate revenue
   B the importance of proper cash levels
   C how to keep from being bought out
   D how to avoid a zero cash balance

2 The woman thinks they should
   A buy out a competitor.
   B invest to generate revenue.
   C operate with a zero cash balance.
   D prepare for unexpected expenses.

7 🎧 Listen again and complete the conversation.

Accountant 2:	I'm glad we have so much cash in reserve.
Accountant 1:	Really? Don't you think it's excessive?
Accountant 2:	Well, no. I think we need that **1** _____ in case something unexpected happens.
Accountant 1:	What are you thinking of?
Accountant 2:	Well, I heard that one of our competitors' sales are plummeting. Maybe we can **2** _____ _____ _____ .
Accountant 1:	I **3** _____ _____ _____ . But in my opinion, it's not good to have that much cash **4** _____ _____ .
Accountant 2:	You think it's unproductive?
Accountant 1:	Exactly. Why not invest it in **5** _____ _____ _____ generate revenue?
Accountant 2:	Hmm ...The way I see it, it's better to **6** _____ _____ and prepared for unexpected expenses.
Accountant 1:	Well, **7** _____ _____ _____ _____ have a zero cash balance.

Speaking

8 With a partner, act out the roles below based on Task 7. Then switch roles.

> **USE LANGUAGE SUCH AS:**
> *Don't you think it's excessive?*
> *I see your point. But in my opinion ...*
> *The way I see it ...*

Student A: You're an accountant. Talk to Student B about:
- cash in reserve
- an excessive amount
- other ways to use it

Student B: You are an accountant. Answer Student A's questions.

Writing

9 Use the conversation from Task 8 to complete the email. Make up names for the CFO and the CPA.

FROM: _____ _____ , CFO
TO: _____ _____ , CPA
RE: cash in reserve

I have a suggestion for a better use of the money that we currently have in reserve. _____
_____
_____
_____

Thank you for considering my idea.

Cordially,
_____ _____

5 Intangible Assets

Accounting Trends Magazine – SPRING ISSUE

Intangible Assets
by Alan Scalin

You are familiar with tangible assets. Any physical object with value is a tangible asset. This includes computers, vehicles, and buildings. There are also assets that do not exist physically. These are **intangible assets**. **Patent rights**, **goodwill**, and **trade secrets** are intangible assets. They are not physical objects. But they are valuable.

There are two types of intangible assets:

Legal intangibles – The law protects these. Patents, **copyrights**, and **trademarks** are legal intangibles.

Competitive intangibles – The most important competitive intangible is called goodwill. This includes valuable factors like a company's reputation, popularity, and location.

Not all intangible assets last forever. For example, patents and copyrights expire. Accountants adjust for this by a process similar to depreciation. It is called **amortization**. They amortize the assets on a straight-line schedule. Other assets, like goodwill, have no time limit. • • •

patent rights

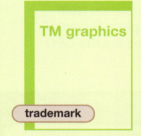
trademark

copyright

trade secrets

Get ready!

1 Before you read the passage, talk about these questions.

1. What are some assets that are not physical objects?
2. How do accountants record these assets?

Reading

2 Read the magazine article. Then, mark the following statements as true (T) or false (F).

1. __ Goodwill is a tangible asset.
2. __ Copyrights have no time limits.
3. __ Trademarks are protected by law.

Vocabulary

3 Match the words or phrases (1-5) with the definitions (A-E).

1. __ trade secret
2. __ patent right
3. __ goodwill
4. __ copyright
5. __ amortization

A the legal protection of an idea or invention
B the gradual reduction of the value of an asset
C knowledge such as recipes or designs
D the legal protection of written materials
E reputation, popularity, and location

4 Choose the sentence that uses the underlined part correctly.

1. A Wages and salaries are considered <u>intangible assets</u>.
   B Andrew's new recipe is protected as a <u>legal intangible</u>.
2. A Knowledge and experience are <u>intangible assets</u>.
   B Recipes and formulas are protected by <u>trademark</u> law.
3. A Location is a <u>competitive intangible</u>.
   B Executive bonuses are considered <u>legal intangibles</u>.
4. A Competitive intangibles protect against <u>unfair competition</u>.
   B A company's symbol is protected as a <u>trademark</u>.

5 🎧 Listen and read the magazine article again. What does goodwill consist of?

Listening

6 🎧 Listen to a conversation between a controller and a potential buyer. Choose the correct answers.

1. What is the dialogue mostly about?
   A a company's location
   B a company's total value
   C a transfer of human capital
   D a group of loyal customers

2. Which of the following is NOT an intangible asset?
   A the company's location
   B the company's reputation
   C the company's annual sales
   D the company's regular customers

7 🎧 Listen again and complete the conversation.

Buyer: I have some questions about your company.
Controller: OK. I'd be happy to answer them.
Buyer: I see **1** _____ _____ _____ your company at one million dollars.
Controller: Right. That's what we **2** _____ _____ _____ from selling it.
Buyer: But you **3** _____ _____ _____ of $500,000 per year. Why do you think the company's worth a million?
Controller: We **4** _____ _____ _____ of intangible assets.
Buyer: Really? **5** _____ _____ ?
Controller: Well, our company **6** _____ _____ _____ this location for almost a hundred years.
Buyer: That's worth something. But in my opinion, it's not worth half a million.

Speaking

8 With a partner, act out the roles below based on Task 7. Then switch roles.

USE LANGUAGE SUCH AS:
Why do you think ...?
We have a lot of intangible assets.
That's worth something. But in my opinion ...

Student A: You are considering buying a company. Talk to Student B about:
- its value
- tangible assets
- intangible assets

Student B: You are a controller at the company. Answer Student A's questions.

Writing

9 Use the conversation from Task 8 to complete the letter. Make up a name for the CPA.

To: James Kent, Owner, Kent Investments

Mr. Kent,

I spoke to the controller from Denver Toy Company. I recommend that you purchase the company. Here's why.

_____
_____
_____
_____

Sincerely,

_____, CPA

6 Presenting a P & L Statement

Profit and Loss Statement
Division A1

	Year Ended December 31, 2010		Year Ended December 31, 2009	
Sales Volume	100,000		100,000	
	Per Unit	Totals	Per Unit	Totals
Sales Revenue	$500	$500,000	$450	$450,000
Cost of Goods Sold	$250	$250,000	$300	$300,000
Gross Margin	$250	$250,000	$150	$150,000
Operating Expenses	$50	$50,000	$50	$50,000
Margin	$200	$200,000	$100	$100,00
Fixed Expenses		$75,000		$75,000
EBIT		$125,000		$25,000

MEMO

From: Kevin Baker, Senior Managerial Accountant
To: Board of Directors

2015 was an excellent year, particularly for Division A1. On the left you'll see their P & L statement. Their **operating earnings** increased from $25,000 in 2014 to $125,000 in 2015. How did they do it?

As you can see, the **sales volume**, **fixed expenses**, and **variable expenses** did not change. Two factors did: cost of goods sold and sales revenue. Let me explain.

In 2014, **wholesalers** were selling our units to **retailers** at a 300% markup. Division A1 managers saw that and raised our price from $450 to $500 in 2015.

Then, in February 2015, one of our primary suppliers lowered its prices. As a result, our cost of goods sold dropped from $300 per unit to just $250.

These factors altered the Division A1 **profit center**. Both **margin per unit** and **total margin** were doubled from 2014 to 2015. The resulting **earning before interest and tax (EBIT)** were the best in the company's history.

Get ready!

1 Before you read the passage, talk about these questions.

1 What are some of the key points on a P & L statement?
2 How do managers use P & L statements?

Reading

2 Read the P & L statement and memo. Then, choose the correct answers.

1 What is the passage mainly about?
   A low operating earnings
   B reasons for increased EBIT
   C errors in a P & L statement
   D proposed changes in division A1

2 Which of the following changed year over year?
   A sales volume   C variable expenses
   B fixed expenses   D cost of goods sold

3 Division A1 managers raised prices because
   A the profit center was diminishing.
   B operating expenses skyrocketed.
   C one of the suppliers raised its prices.
   D wholesalers could absorb the increase.

Vocabulary

3 Match the words or phrases (1-4) with the definitions (A-D).

1 __ operating earnings   3 __ total margin
2 __ fixed expenses   4 __ wholesaler

A sales revenue minus variable expenses
B costs that do not change from month to month
C a company that distributes products to retailers
D the money retained after fixed and variable expenses

4 Read the sentence pairs. Choose which word or phrase best fits each blank.

1. variable expenses / retailers
   A _____ sell products to the public.
   B _____ often change each month.

2. profit center / margin per unit
   A A _____ is a money-making division within a company.
   B _____ is the revenue per product after variable expenses.

3. sales volume / earnings before interest and tax
   A The total number of products sold is called _____.
   B Revenue minus fixed and variable expenses is _____.

5 🎧 Listen and read the statement and memo again. What factors caused the increase in EBIT from 2014 to 2015?

Listening

6 🎧 Listen to a conversation between an accountant and a director. Mark the following statements as true (T) or false (F).

1. __ The company's earnings dropped in 2015.
2. __ The company's costs went down while prices went up.
3. __ The wholesalers lowered their prices to retailers.

7 🎧 Listen again and complete the conversation.

Director: I'm impressed. We've never had such a huge increase in a profit center.
Controller: I know. We really got lucky in 2015.
Director: I'm sorry, what do you mean by that?
Controller: I mean that 1 _____ _____ _____ something like that.
Director: Why not? I think the managers 2 _____ _____ _____ _____ raising the price.
Controller: They did. The wholesalers were making huge profits and we 3 _____ _____ _____ some of that for ourselves.
Director: Can we 4 _____ _____ _____ to other divisions?
Controller: We can. But they wouldn't have such a 5 _____ _____ in EBIT unless another supplier lowered their prices.
Director: Ah, I see what you mean 6 _____ _____. We can't predict when that might happen.

Speaking

8 With a partner, act out the roles below based on Task 7. Then switch roles.

USE LANGUAGE SUCH AS:
I'm impressed. We've never had ...
We really got lucky ...
I'm sorry. What do you mean by that?

Student A: You are a director. Talk to Student B about:
- increased earnings
- causes
- can it be repeated

Student B: You are a controller. Answer Student A's questions.

Writing

9 Use the conversation from Task 8 to complete the memo.

MEMO

To: Management and Accounting Staff

Earnings went way up on our last P & L statement. There are a few reasons for this and a few ways we can try to have similar success in the future. _____
_____
_____
_____
_____
_____

7 Internal Controls Against Mistakes and Theft

Get ready!

1 Before you read the passage, talk about these questions.

1. What are some crimes that take place in the accounting profession?
2. How can organizations guard against these crimes?

shoplift

falsification

Small Business Quarterly

Accountability in the Accounting Profession
by Victoria Harris

Fraud, **forgery**, and **embezzlement** are entertaining when they happen in a detective movie. But in real life, they are serious problems. Businesses lose thousands of dollars every year to these crimes. This is one reason accounting requires so much paperwork.

Paperwork and other **accounting controls** are necessary. They minimize crime and **deceit**. Threats come from inside and outside a business. Even managers and other businesses must be **held accountable**. Customers **shoplift**. Suppliers short-ship. Managers accept **kick-backs**. How can these activities be prevented?

Here are a few important accounting controls:

- Require two signatures on any cash disbursement. This guards against **misappropriation**.
- Conduct surprise inventory audits. This helps to detect **pilfering** and **falsification** of records.
- Require two managers to approve any write-offs. This prevents kick-backs and fraud.
- Rotate employees. Instruct them to watch for suspicious activity.
- Match all receiving reports with the general ledger. This prevents short-counts.

...

pilfering

Reading

2 Read the article from an accounting journal. Then, choose the correct answers.

1. What is the passage mainly about?
   A a famous kick-back case
   B methods for avoiding crime
   C falsification of personal records
   D reasons why theft prevention fails

2. How can an organization prevent misappropriation?
   A conduct nightly inventory audits
   B have three managers approve write-offs
   C require two signatures on cash disbursements
   D match receiving reports with the packing slips

3. Which of the following is NOT an internal threat?
   A pilfering   C shoplifting
   B kick-backs   D misappropriation

Vocabulary

3 Match the words or phrases (1-5) with the definitions (A-E).

1 __ embezzle   4 __ hold accountable
2 __ falsification   5 __ kick-back
3 __ misappropriation

A to take company resources for personal use
B the act of delivering money to the wrong recipient
C a bribe that is paid in return for favorable treatment
D the act of putting false information in company records
E to require that people be responsible for their actions

4 Read the sentence pairs. Choose which word or phrase best fits each blank.

1 fraud / accounting controls
   A Companies can fight crime using _____.
   B _____ is the act of gaining money by deceit.

2 forgery / shoplifting
   A It looked like Karen's signature, but it was a _____.
   B The store has security guards to watch for _____.

3 deceit / pilfering
   A Falsification, lying, or any other _____ will get you fired.
   B If the inventory is short, it's possible someone was _____.

5 🎧 Listen and read the article again. What are some internal and external threats to a business?

Listening

6 🎧 Listen to a conversation between two accountants. Mark the following statements as true (T) or false (F).

1 __ Some employees were pilfering.
2 __ The general ledger contained an error.
3 __ The receiving clerks must write new purchase orders.

7 🎧 Listen again and complete the conversation.

Accountant 1:	I just found out we have a major problem with inventory fraud.
Accountant 2:	Really? How do you know?
Accountant 1:	I compared the actual inventory to what is recorded in our general ledger. We're missing a lot of inventory.
Accountant 2:	Oh, no. Do you think some of the employees are **1** _____?
Accountant 1:	That **2** _____ _____ _____ _____ the problem. I think some of the suppliers have been short-shipping.
Accountant 2:	OK. What do you think we should do about it?
Accountant 1:	**3** _____ _____ _____ someone match every receiving report with the purchase orders?
Accountant 2:	That's a good idea. And we can also have the receiving **4** _____ _____ _____ of any shipments that are short of product.
Accountant 1:	That **5** _____ _____ to me. I'll write a **6** _____ _____ _____ about the purchase orders.
Accountant 2:	All right. I'll **7** _____ _____ _____ _____ with the receiving clerks.

Speaking

8 With a partner, act out the roles below based on Task 7. Then switch roles.

USE LANGUAGE SUCH AS:
I just found out we have a major problem with ...
Do you think some employees are ...?
How about ...?

Student A: You are an accountant. Talk to Student B about:
• fraud
• who is committing it
• how to stop it

Student B: You are an accountant. Answer Student A's questions.

Writing

9 Use the conversation from Task 8 to complete the memo.

MEMO

RE: preventing fraud

Here are some steps that we want everyone to take to prevent fraud.

_____
_____
_____
_____
_____

17

8 Accrual Basis Accounting – Non-cash Accounts

cash-basis accounting

PAID IN ADVANCE
paid ahead of time

Accrual Basis Accounting – Non-Cash Accounts

Some businesses use cash basis accounting. They record every amount of cash that they receive or spend. But many businesses use another method called **accrual basis accounting**.

Here are three types of accrual basis non-cash accounts:

Accounts receivable – Many companies make sales **on credit**. The cash from these sales is received later. But the sale is still recorded in **accounts receivable**.

Accounts payable – Companies also make purchases on credit. The payment for these purchases is made later. But the amounts are recorded immediately in **accounts payable**.

Prepaid expense – This covers products or services that are **paid for ahead of time**. For example, a business may purchase insurance policies that require a year or more **advance payment**. The business records this payment as a **prepaid expense asset**. Then they **allocate** it to their expense accounts in monthly **increments**.

on credit

Get ready!

1 Before you read the passage, talk about these questions.

1 What are some transactions that don't involve cash?
2 How do accountants record these transactions?

Reading

2 Read the textbook passage. Then, choose the correct answers.

1 What is the passage mainly about?
 A how to account for non-cash assets
 B what items to pay for ahead of time
 C how to use a new type of accounting
 D what purchases can be made on credit

2 Prepaid expenses are
 A a type of payable account.
 B non-cash accounts that involve credit.
 C allocated to expense accounts monthly.
 D a good option with cash basis accounting.

3 Cash basis accounting
 A is a good way to increase cash.
 B records only the exchange of cash.
 C is more accurate than accrual basis.
 D does not record advance payments.

Vocabulary

3 Match the words or phrases (1-4) with the definitions (A-D).

1 __ on credit   3 __ advance payment
2 __ increment   4 __ allocate

A a small amount delivered periodically
B to pay for something prior to receiving it
C to purchase something and pay for it later
D to assign something to a particular location

4 Read the sentence pairs. Choose which word or phrase best fits each blank.

1. accounts receivable / paid for ahead of time
   A The insurance policy must be _____.
   B _____ will cover those expenses.

2. accrual basis accounting / accounts payable
   A _____ is more flexible than cash basis.
   B Credit purchases are recorded in _____.

3. cash basis accounting / prepaid expense assets
   A _____ are expenses that are paid in advance.
   B _____ records only the exchange of cash.

5 🎧 Listen and read the textbook passage again. What are the 3 kinds of accrual basis accounts?

Listening

6 🎧 Listen to a conversation between an accountant and her client. Mark the following statements as true (T) or false (F).

1. __ The man chooses cash basis accounting.
2. __ Accrual basis accounting follows cash flow.
3. __ There are delays with accrual basis accounting.

7 🎧 Listen again and complete the conversation.

Accountant: So, you wanted to talk about accounting methods?
Client: Yes. I'm not sure if I should use cash basis or accrual basis accounting.
Accountant: OK. Well, cash basis accounting is good for tracking cash flow.
Client: That makes sense. It's because you only **1** _____ _____ when cash is exchanged, right.
Accountant: Exactly. But accrual basis accounting is better for **2** _____ _____ and expenses.
Client: What do you mean by that?
Accountant: Well, **3** _____ _____ _____ with cash flow. You might **4** _____ _____ _____ but not receive cash for a month.
Client: Oh, I see. But with accrual basis accounting I could record that **5** _____ _____.
Accountant: That's right. So, **6** _____ _____ _____ _____?
Client: Well, I'd rather **7** _____ _____ _____ _____ cash flow. Let's use cash basis accounting.

Speaking

8 With a partner, act out the dialogue from Task 7. Then switch roles.

USE LANGUAGE SUCH AS:

So you wanted to talk about accounting methods?
I'm not sure if I should use ...
Well, cash basis accounting is good for ...

Student A: You are opening a business. Talk to Student B about:
- accounting methods
- advantages/disadvantages
- your preference

Student B: You are an accountant. Answer Student A's questions.

Writing

9 Use the conversation from Task 8 to complete the business owner's notes.

Notes

Cash basis accounting

_____
_____
_____
_____

Accrual basis accounting

_____
_____
_____
_____

19

9 Unpaid Expenses

Get ready!

1 Before you read the passage, talk about these questions.

1. What are some expenses that a business doesn't pay right away?
2. How do accountants record these expenses?

Unpaid Expenses

Sometimes businesses must record an expense, but don't have to pay it right away. How do they keep track of these unpaid expenses? They can account for them **via** two types of payable accounts:

Income tax payable – Sometimes, a business owes taxes for a certain year that are not due until the following year. The unpaid amount is recorded in an income tax payable account and paid in increments throughout the following year.

Accrued expenses payable – Businesses have to calculate and record expenses for which they have not been **billed**:

- Unused vacation days that **carry over** to the following year
- Interest that isn't due until the end of a **loan period**
- **Bonuses** owed to executives and salespeople

These **accruals** are made throughout the year and recorded in an accrued expenses payable account.

accruals

Reading

2 Read the textbook passage. Then, mark the following statements as true (T) or false (F).

1. __ Unused vacation days are lost at the end of the year.
2. __ Income tax payable is settled via incremental payments.
3. __ Accrued expenses payable carry over from year to year.

Vocabulary

3 Match the words or phrases (1-4) with the definitions (A-D).

1. __ bill
2. __ loan period
3. __ carry over
4. __ accruals

A to transfer an amount from one period to another
B the length of time for repaying borrowed money
C a document stating what is owed
D amounts that are accumulated over time

4 Fill in the blanks with the correct words or phrases from the word bank.

Word BANK

via   bonus   income tax payable
accrued expense payable

1. Calculate this year's taxes and record the amount in _____ .
2. Debt payments are made _____ the cash account.
3. If salespeople reach their target, they will get a(n) _____ .
4. Unused vacation days must be recorded as a(n) _____ .

5 🎧 Listen and read the textbook passage again. What should a company do with an unbilled expense?

Listening

6 🎧 Listen to a conversation between two accountants. Choose the correct answers.

1 What is the dialogue mostly about?
   A raising executive salaries
   B recording an accrued expense
   C creating a new expense account
   D settling last year's expense accounts

2 According to the dialogue, bonuses are
   A the same every year.
   B given to accountants.
   C paid at the end of the year.
   D estimated according to sales.

7 🎧 Listen again and complete the conversation.

Accountant 1:	Larry, could you help me, with these expense accounts?
Accountant 2:	Sure, Vicky, what's up?
Accountant 1:	I need to know how to account for bonuses.
Accountant 2:	You mean the bonuses we pay to **1** _____ _____ _____ ?
Accountant 1:	Right. We **2** _____ _____ _____ until the **3** _____ _____ _____ _____ , so how do I know how much they will be?
Accountant 2:	Well, you **4** _____ _____ _____ _____ know. I can give you estimates.
Accountant 1:	How do you estimate them?
Accountant 2:	I use the amounts of **5** _____ _____ _____ as a guide.
Accountant 1:	OK. **6** _____ _____ _____ . But the amounts vary every year, right?
Accountant 2:	They do. The estimates won't be **7** _____ _____ , but that's not a problem.
Accountant 1:	So then, how do I record them?
Accountant 2:	You need to record them in the accrued expenses payable account.

Speaking

8 With a partner, act out the roles below based on Task 7. Then switch roles.

USE LANGUAGE SUCH AS:
How do I know how much ...?
You don't actually have to know ...
How do you estimate ...?

Student A: You are an accountant. Talk to Student B about:
• bonuses
• estimates
• recording them

Student B: You are an accountant. Answer Student A's questions.

Writing

9 Use the conversation from Task 8 to complete the memo.

MEMO

TO: accountants

RE: bonuses

Bonuses are paid to salespeople and executives at the end of the year. We account for this by

_____
_____
_____
_____
_____

21

10 Leverage — Good or Bad?

LEVERAGE: Use What You Have

BUSINESS TODAY - JULY 2011

For months you've been thinking about getting a new office in a nicer part of town. You already own the land; you just need to build the office. But there's one problem: you don't have enough cash. What can you do?

You can **leverage** the land. In other words, use the land as **collateral** and **take out** a loan to build the office. There is a risk, of course. The lender will have a **senior claim** on your property. If you **default**, the lender will take your land and the building. Be careful when you choose a loan — not all loans are created equal.

There are good loans and bad loans. Don't take a loan unless it has **desirable terms**. Shop around until you find one with a low **interest rate**, low fees, a reasonable **origination fee**, and **tax deductible** interest. You should also look for one that you can **pay off** early without penalties. ...

Get ready!

1 Before you read the passage, talk about these questions.

1 Why do businesses take out loans?
2 How can businesses raise needed capital?

Reading

2 Read the article from a business magazine. Then, mark the following statements as true (T) or false (F).

1 __ Owners keep senior claims on their leveraged property.
2 __ There are many types of loans with varying terms.
3 __ The interest on some loans can help lower taxes.

Vocabulary

3 Match the words or phrases (1-5) with the definitions (A-E).

1 __ leverage   4 __ default
2 __ desirable terms   5 __ interest rate
3 __ origination fee

A to fail to make payments
B a percentage added to a loan amount yearly
C the fee for making a loan
D to use an asset as collateral
E favorable conditions

4 Fill in the blanks with the correct words or phrases from the word bank.

WORD BANK

tax deductible   collateral   pay off   senior claim   take out

1. Having _____ interest is a great way to lower tax bills.
2. The company must _____ its debts before borrowing more.
3. Defaulting on the loan would result in the loss of _____ .
4. The bank has a _____ on the company's building.
5. A bad economy forced the company to _____ another loan.

5 🎧 Listen and read the article again. What are some attractive terms to look for when considering a bank loan?

Listening

6 🎧 Listen to a conversation between an accountant and her client. Choose the correct answers.

1. What is the dialogue mostly about?
   - A taking out a loan
   - B renegotiating terms
   - C financing a new business
   - D making an early payment

2. What will the man likely do?
   - A change his business plans
   - B try to get a loan elsewhere
   - C pay off some of his business's debts
   - D ask for another accountant's opinion

7 🎧 Listen again and complete the conversation.

Client: I met with a banker yesterday and got a loan offer.
Accountant: That's great! What are the terms?
Client: The fees and interest rate are really low.
Accountant: Good. Now will the interest be tax deductible?
Client: It will. The only negative is that they said something about **1** _____ _____ _____ in 5 years.
Accountant: Oh, that's not a good thing.
Client: No, but all the **2** _____ _____ are great.
Accountant: Hmm ... **3** _____ _____ _____ for paying it off early?
Client: Oh, yeah, I **4** _____ _____ _____ that. There are. But I don't plan to **5** _____ _____ _____ _____ , so it's OK.
Accountant: Well, what if your business **6** _____ _____ _____ and you want to get rid of some debt?
Client: That's a good point. Maybe I should **7** _____ _____ .

Speaking

8 With a partner, act out the roles below based on Task 7. Then switch roles.

USE LANGUAGE SUCH AS:

I met with a banker and got a loan offer.

What are the terms?

That's great/not good.

Student A: You are taking out a loan. Talk to Student B about:
- the terms
- his/her recommendation

Student B: You are an accountant. Answer Student A's questions.

Writing

9 Use the conversation from Task 8 to complete the letter. Make up names for the client and the CPA

Mr. _____ ,

I am writing in regards to the loan papers you asked me to review. I recommend that you don't take this loan offer. Let me explain why.

_____
_____
_____
_____
_____
_____

Sincerely,

_____ , CPA

23

11 Variable Expenses

employee benefits

equipment failure

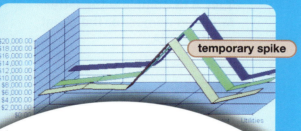
temporary spike

FUTURE TECH
DEVELOPMENT CORPORATION

2010 Variable Expense Report

Variable expenses rose dramatically in 2014. Several factors contributed to this rise.

Employee Benefits – In February, we increased our contributions to the employees' retirement plan. This resulted in a 5% rise in our employee benefits cost.

Advertising – Advertising costs skyrocketed from $10,000 in March to $30,000 in April. This was due to the launching of a new TV commercial **campaign**.

Charitable Contributions – In May, after several months of steadily rising profits, we increased charitable contributions by 2%.

Repairs – In July, equipment failures resulted in a **temporary spike** in expenses. All repairs were completed by August and our expenses **leveled off**.

Profit Sharing Plan – In September, the Board of Directors **discontinued** the profit sharing plan due to declining sales revenue.

Compensation of Officers – We promised executives in every department a 5% bonus on any revenue generated over the previous year's revenue. Sales skyrocketed in 2014. As a result, $100,000 was paid in bonuses from October through December.

Get ready!

1 Before you read the passage, talk about these questions.

1. What expenses can change from month to month?
2. What causes these expenses to rise or fall?

Reading

2 Read the report. Then, mark the following statements as true (T) or false (F).

1. __ The company increased contributions to the profit sharing plan.
2. __ Revenue in 2014 was less than it was in 2013.
3. __ Advertising expenditures rose by 200% from March to April.

Vocabulary

3 Match the words or phrases (1-5) with the definitions (A-E).

1. __ repairs
2. __ level off
3. __ spike
4. __ charitable
5. __ profit sharing plan

A done to help other people
B fixing something that is broken
C a sharp, dramatic rise
D giving employees part of a company's revenue
E to stop rising or falling

4. Fill in the blanks with the correct words or phrases from the word bank.

Word BANK

discontinue   temporary   campaign   employee benefits

1. The economic downturn is not permanent; it's _____.
2. Our competition is running a strong _____ of radio ads.
3. Lack of funding forced the company to _____ the program.
4. Henry's job has health insurance and a lot of other great _____.

5. Listen and read the report again. Which costs decreased in 2010?

Listening

6. Listen to a conversation between a controller and a CFO. Choose the correct answers.

1. What is the dialogue mostly about?
   - A explaining a report
   - B increasing bonuses
   - C limiting advertising costs
   - D generating income for a charity

2. The man thinks that TV advertising
   - A will be stopped.
   - B should focus on charity.
   - C caused profits to increase.
   - D wasn't approved by executives.

7. Listen again and complete the conversation.

Controller: Did you see my report on last year's expenses?
CFO: I did. We really had a **1** _____ in overall variable expenses, didn't we?
Controller: Yes, we did. How do you feel about that?
CFO: Well, most of it is pretty **2** _____ , but the advertising ... how could it go up so much?
Controller: Yeah, that's a pretty **3** _____ .
CFO: No kidding. From $10,000 to $30,000 — that's huge!
Controller: Well, TV advertising is expensive, but **4** _____ .
CFO: That's true. I think the **5** _____ covered the expense.
Controller: It did. And it **6** _____ that we were able to increase our **7** _____ .

Speaking

8. With a partner, act out the roles below based on Task 7. Then switch roles.

USE LANGUAGE SUCH AS:
We really had a huge increase in ...
How do you feel about that?
Do you think we'll ...?

Student A: You are a controller. Talk to Student B about:
- increases or decreases in variable expenses
- reasons for changes

Student B: You are a CFO. Answer Student A's questions.

Writing

9. Use the conversation from Task 8 to complete the letter. Make up names for the CFO and the president.

From: _____ , CFO
To: _____ , President

Ms. _____ ,

As you know, our variable expenses rose considerably last year. But this is nothing to be concerned about. Let me explain.

_____
_____
_____
_____

Best wishes,

_____ , CFO

25

12 End-of-Period Procedures

out of the ordinary

Get ready!

1 Before you read the passage, talk about these questions.

1. What are end-of-period procedures?
2. What are some problems that might occur during end-of-period procedures?

red flag

From: George Garcia, CPA, Benjamin Landon and Associates
To: Cynthia Hall, CFO, Bedford Express Plastics

Miss Hall,

I have completed the end-of-period procedures for your business. Although there were a lot more transactions this period, I did not have to make very many **adjusting entries**. This made it easier for me. Your new bookkeepers did an excellent job recording the day-to-day **flow of transactions**. Their accounting was accurate and they left very detailed **audit trails**.

However, as I was making a last minute **sweep** of all your records, I noticed something **out of the ordinary**. You have an **abnormally** large balance in the receivable account for your customer, Gentle Giant Manufacturing. It first **caught my attention** when I saw that the company did not make a payment through the entire period. It's one of your regular customers, right? I find it hard to believe that Gentle Giant would try to **stiff** you. However, this is definitely a **red flag**, and you might want to look into it.

Best Wishes,
George

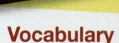
sweep

Reading

2 Read the email. Then, mark the following statements as true (T) or false (F).

1. __ The bookkeepers made errors in a receivable account.
2. __ The business experienced an increase of transactions.
3. __ Gentle Giant created audit trails.

Vocabulary

3 Match the words or phrases (1-5) with the definitions (A-E).

1. __ red flag
2. __ sweep
3. __ abnormally
4. __ stiff
5. __ audit trails

A detailed records that are easy to study
B a detail that is alarming
C to fail to pay someone for goods or services
D a study of an area or a set of information
E odd; out of the ordinary

4 Fill in the blanks with the correct phrases from the word bank.

word BANK

caught my attention   flow of transactions
out of the ordinary   adjusting entries

1. The records had errors, so Jacob made _____.
2. The errors were _____, usually the bookkeepers are very careful.
3. The obvious errors quickly _____.
4. The _____ slowed in the bad economy.

5 🎧 Listen and read the email again. What concern is brought to the attention of the CFO?

Listening

6 🎧 Listen to a conversation between an accountant and his client. Choose the correct answers.

1. What is the dialogue mostly about?
   - A a red flag
   - B new procedures
   - C early payments
   - D a long-time customer

2. What does the man think about Thomas and Nash Distributing?
   - A It is a new customer.
   - B It had an accounting error.
   - C It is going to stiff his client.
   - D It owes the client a lot of money.

7 🎧 Listen again and complete the conversation.

Client: Is something wrong?
Accountant: Maybe. See, you have a really big **1** _____ _____ for one of your customers.
Client: Have they **2** _____ _____ _____ payments?
Accountant: No. They've only made one payment **3** _____ _____ _____.
Client: Is it Thompson and Nash Distributing?
Accountant: Yes. **4** _____ _____ _____ they are going to stiff you. I'm just saying it's **5** _____ _____ _____ _____.
Client: Actually, I talked to their CFO last week. Their payments **6** _____ _____ because of an accounting error.
Accountant: Oh, I see. **7** _____ _____ _____.

Speaking

8 With a partner, act out the roles below based on Task 7. Then switch roles.

USE LANGUAGE SUCH AS:
Is something wrong?
Maybe. You have a ...
I talked to their CFO last week.

Student A: You are a client meeting with your accountant. Talk to Student B about:
- end-of-period procedures
- problems
- solutions

Student B: You are an accountant. Answer Student A's questions.

Writing

9 Use the conversation from Task 8 to complete the email.

FROM: _____ _____, Owner
TO: _____ _____, CPA

I got your message. You are right. The amount in _____ seems a little off. I spoke to their CFO las week. Here's the problem: _____
_____
_____
_____

Thanks for all your hard work!

Best wishes,

_____

27

13 Accounting Software

PBL UNLIMITED

It's here! The new version of PBL's complete accounting software offers the same **ease of use**, **security**, and **functionality** as our previous version, plus **updates** to launch your business into the future of financial accounting.

PBL Unlimited features:
- Up to 50 **user licenses**
- Cash flow manager
- Automatic inventory tracking
- Audit trail report
- **Remote access**
- **Data mining**
- Unlimited customer accounts
- Two years of free updates
- And so much more ...

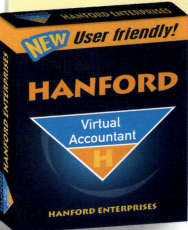

HANFORD Virtual Accountant

Are you tired of paying hundreds of dollars in accountant fees?
Do you wish there was a simpler and cheaper way?

With the Virtual Accountant, there is!

The Virtual Accountant is Hanford Enterprises' new **user-friendly** accounting software designed especially for individuals and small businesses. This simple program will help you get your accounting operations **up and running**. It includes simple tutorials to show you how to manage your data and avoid "**garbage in, garbage out**."

Call today to talk to a Hanford representative!

Get ready!

1 Before you read the passage, talk about these questions.

1. What are the advantages to using accounting software?
2. What are some different types of accounting software?

Reading

2 Read these advertisements. Then, mark the following statements as true (T) or false (F).

1. __ Multiple users can operate PBL Unlimited.
2. __ The Virtual Accountant features self-teaching tools.
3. __ The Virtual Accountant is best for large firms.

Vocabulary

3 Match the words or phrases (1-5) with the definitions (A-E).

1. __ ease of use
2. __ updates
3. __ garbage in, garbage out
4. __ functionality
5. __ data mining

A. the result of flawed input is flawed output
B. improvements created by a program's designers
C. analyzing information and finding patterns in it
D. the degree to which a program is simple to operate
E. the degree to which a program is practical and useful

4 Fill in the blanks with the correct words or phrases: *user licenses, remote access, up and running, tutorials, user-friendly.*

1 Large firms need software with a lot of _____ .
2 The business will be _____ soon.
3 Don is travelling and wants a program with _____ .
4 Individuals may want a program that is _____ .
5 People who are new to accounting should use _____ .

5 🎧 Listen and read the advertisement again. How many people are allowed to use one copy of PBL unlimited?

Listening

6 🎧 Listen to a conversation between two accountants. Choose the correct answers.

1 What is the dialogue mostly about?
   A choosing software
   B the number of users
   C PBL's latest update
   D using outdated software

2 What are the accountants likely to do?
   A stop using software
   B select PBL Unlimited
   C shop for other programs
   D update their current software

7 🎧 Listen again and complete the conversation.

Accountant 1:	So, Tim, have you thought about which **1** _____ _____ we should get?
Accountant 2:	Well, I'm thinking about getting PBL Unlimited.
Accountant 1:	Hmm ... I **2** _____ _____ PBL Unlimited. I like the Virtual Accountant, though.
Accountant 2:	This **3** _____ _____ PBL Unlimited has some **4** _____ _____ _____ .
Accountant 1:	But the Virtual Accountant is really easy to use. It has tutorials on **5** _____ _____ _____ .
Accountant 2:	That's cool. But I **6** _____ _____ _____ for homes, not businesses.
Accountant 1:	You don't think it would work for the business?
Accountant 2:	Well, I would **7** _____ _____ _____ something with more features.
Accountant 1:	What features does PBL Unlimited have?
Accountant 2:	Oh, it has everything! It has inventory tracking, data mining and a lot more.

Speaking

8 With a partner, act out the roles below based on Task 7. Then switch roles.

USE LANGUAGE SUCH AS:
Have you thought about which software ...?
I'm thinking about getting ...
I would prefer to get ...

Student A: You are an accountant. Talk to Student B about:
* software
* features
* preferences

Student B: You are an accountant. Answer Student A's questions.

Writing

9 Use the advertisement and the conversation from Task 8 to complete the email.

FROM: _____ _____ , CPA
TO: _____ _____ , Accounting Manager

I know you want to buy new software for our department. I just wanted to let you know about a really great program that I used at a previous job. _____
_____
_____
_____
_____

Thanks for your time!
_____

14 Reporting Extraordinary Gains and Losses

Business and Finance Weekly – Oct. 15

Accounting for the Extraordinary
— *by Scott Unser*

Wouldn't it be nice if life were always predictable? Especially in business, it would be wonderful to know exactly what was going to happen. But that's not reality. Unexpected **extraordinary** gains and losses happen for various reasons. You must record any gains and write off any losses.

Here are some examples of events that cause financial **discontinuity**:

Abandoning product lines
– If you stop selling a product that you still have in inventory, you may have to sell the inventory at a discounted price.

Damaged or impaired assets
– If an asset is damaged and cannot be used, or **impaired** in its usefulness, this loss must be written off.

Downsizing and restructuring
– If you **layoff** employees, you have to pay them **severance packages**. This can result in an extraordinary loss.

Lawsuits
– You may be required to pay **damages** or fines, resulting in an extraordinary loss. Or, you may be owed damages, resulting in an extraordinary gain.

...

Get ready!

1 Before you read the passage, talk about these questions.

1 When do businesses experience extraordinary gains or losses?
2 How do accountants report these figures in your country?

Reading

2 Read this article from an accounting journal. Then, mark the following statements as true (T) or false (F).

1 __ Restructuring involves reducing a workforce.
2 __ Abandoned product lines must be written off.
3 __ Severance packages include damages and fines.

Vocabulary

3 Match the words (1-5) with the definitions (A-E).

1 __ extraordinary   3 __ lawsuit   5 __ layoff
2 __ downsize   4 __ impaired

A unable to fulfill the expected role
B beyond what is normal
C to end someone's employment
D to reduce the size of a business
E a formal legal proceeding

4 Fill in the blanks with the correct words or phrases: *discontinuity*, *restructuring*, *damages*, *severance package*.

1 Cathy was fired, but she got a very generous _____.
2 The company lost the lawsuit and had to pay _____.
3 _____ is any extraordinary gain or loss.
4 The company was very profitable after its _____.

5 🎧 Listen and read the article again. What might you have to do with old product lines?

Listening

6 🎧 Listen to a conversation between two accountants. Choose the correct answers.

1 What is the dialogue mostly about?
   A sending a report to a client
   B fixing mathematical errors
   C reporting unusual expenses
   D compensating for downsizing

2 The woman suggests
   A laying off more employees.
   B increasing severance packages.
   C drafting a new income statement.
   D putting extraordinary gains and losses in a separate section.

7 🎧 Listen again and complete the conversation.

Accountant 1:	Excuse me, Miss Carter, could you look at this income statement I drafted?
Accountant 2:	Sure, Nathan. 1 _____.
Accountant 1:	Thanks. I want 2 _____ I got it right.
Accountant 2:	Um, 3 _____ under expenses? Is that severance packages?
Accountant 1:	Yes it is. 4 _____ when we downsized two months ago.
Accountant 2:	Yes, I remember. We 5 _____. But you can't 6 _____ regular expenses.
Accountant 1:	Really? Why not?
Accountant 2:	Well, if you do, people will see those major losses as a regular expense.
Accountant 1:	So how do you account for them?
Accountant 2:	Well, at the bottom of the statement, put another section called extraordinary gains and losses.

Speaking

8 With a partner, act out the roles below based on Task 7. Then switch roles.

> **USE LANGUAGE SUCH AS:**
> *Could you look at this income statement I drafted?*
> *What's this line under ...?*
> *You can't report those as ...*

Student A: You are an accountant. Talk to Student B about:
- an extraordinary gain/loss
- how to report extraordinary gains/losses

Student B: You are an accountant. Answer Student A's questions.

Writing

9 Use the article and the conversation from Task 8 to complete the memo.

MEMO

RE: Extraordinary gains and losses

There are a few types of extraordinary gains and losses: _____

_____

These amounts need to be reported separately because _____

15 Is Profit Ethical?

Business Today – July, 2011

Is Profit Ethical?

by Gina Knowles

Some people say that profit is **unethical**. They believe that businesses **make a killing** by **exploiting** their workers, many of whom struggle to live above the poverty line. Some say businesses damage the environment as well. And yes, there may be some individuals who take the **low road** and engage in unethical or **immoral** business practices. But the inappropriate actions of a few do not **condemn** all. Most owners operate **ethical**, **environmentally friendly** businesses. Profit is merely a return on effort. As long as it is gained responsibly, showing respect to the Earth and its inhabitants, there is nothing immoral about it.

Furthermore, it's very interesting that businesses are rarely **criticized** for their handling of losses. Who pays for losses? Business owners do. Businesses have potential for profit because they also have great potential for loss. How can anyone say that's unethical?

...

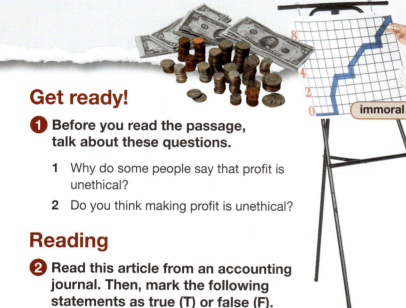

immoral

poverty line

Get ready!

1 Before you read the passage, talk about these questions.

1. Why do some people say that profit is unethical?
2. Do you think making profit is unethical?

Reading

2 Read this article from an accounting journal. Then, mark the following statements as true (T) or false (F).

1. __ Business owners pay for losses.
2. __ Business owners define the poverty line.
3. __ According to the passage, workers exploit businesses.

Vocabulary

3 Match the words or phrases (1-5) with the definitions (A-E).

1. __ unethical
2. __ poverty line
3. __ exploit
4. __ make a killing
5. __ condemn

A to take advantage of someone
B to generate huge profits
C not conforming to moral standards
D to judge someone or something unfavorably
E the amount of income needed to cover basic needs

4 Fill in the blanks with the correct words or phrases from the word bank.

Word BANK

low road   environmentally friendly
immoral   ethical   criticize

1. Making a profit is only _____ if it hurts someone.
2. Some people _____ businesses for making profit.
3. Their _____ policies minimize their effect on the Earth.
4. Making a profit is _____ as long as it's made fairly.
5. Unfortunately, Angela chose to take the _____.

5 🎧 Listen and read the article again. How does it describe profit?

Listening

6 🎧 Listen to a conversation between two accountants. Choose the correct answers.

1. What is the dialogue mostly about?
   A how business owners can fail
   B whether making money is moral
   C what kinds of risks employees face
   D why the poverty line should be moved

2. The woman thinks that owners
   A often take the low road.
   B gain wealth by creating poverty.
   C suffer loss the same as employees.
   D deserve more profit because of risk.

7 🎧 Listen again and complete the conversation.

Accountant 1:	Actually, I think they might **1** _____ _____ _____ _____ .
Accountant 2:	What? Why would you say that?
Accountant 1:	Well, you know, sometimes businesses **2** _____ _____ _____ .
Accountant 2:	Yeah, maybe that happens **3** _____ _____ _____ _____ , but not very often.
Accountant 1:	Some people **4** _____ _____ because they see wealthy owners with employees who **5** _____ _____ _____ the poverty line.
Accountant 2:	But the owners **6** _____ _____ profit because they have more risk.

Speaking

8 With a partner, act out the roles below based on Task 7. Then switch roles.

> **USE LANGUAGE SUCH AS:**
> *I think they might have a good point.*
> *Why would you say that?*
> *Sometimes businesses ...*

Student A: You are an accountant. Talk to Student B about:
- when profit is ethical
- when profit is unethical

Student B: You are an accountant. Answer Student A's questions.

Writing

9 Use the article and the conversation from Task 8 to complete the letter to a magazine editor.

Dear Editor,

I am writing in response to the article about profit that you published last month. The article stated that making a profit is unethical. I [agree / disagree]. Let me explain why.

_____
_____
_____
_____
_____
_____

Sincerely,

_____

33

Glossary

abnormally [ADV-U12] If something is done or exists **abnormally**, it does so without conforming to normal patterns.

accounting control [N-COUNT-U7] An **accounting control** is a procedure designed to prevent crime and/or deceit.

accounting system [N-COUNT-U3] An **accounting system** is a uniform set of methods and procedures.

accounts payable [N-PL-U8] **Accounts payable** are the accounts in which credit purchases are recorded.

accounts receivable [N-PL-U8] **Accounts receivable** are the accounts in which credit sales are recorded.

accrual [N-COUNT-U9] An **accrual** is an amount that is added to a quantity of something.

accrual basis accounting [N-UNCOUNT-U8] **Accrual basis accounting** is an accounting method in which non-cash transactions are recorded.

accrued expenses payable [N-PL-U9] **Accrued expenses payable** are expenses such as bonuses and interest payments that are not due until some later date.

adjusting entry [N-COUNT-U12] An **adjusting entry** is an amount that is recorded to compensate for an error.

advance payment [N-COUNT-U8] An **advance payment** is a payment that is given before the product or service is exchanged.

allocate [V-T-U8] To **allocate** something is to assign it to a particular location.

amortization [N-UNCOUNT-U5] **Amortization** is the process by which the value of certain intangible assets is reduced.

attention to detail [N-UNCOUNT-U3] **Attention to detail** is a characteristic involving focus and precision.

audit trail [N-COUNT-U12] An **audit trail** is a pattern of detailed records that is easy to understand.

background check [N-COUNT-U3] A **background check** is the research into an individual's past to see if that person has a criminal record.

bill [V-T-U9] To **bill** someone is to send him or her a document stating an amount of money that he or she owes.

bonus [N-COUNT-U9] A **bonus** is an amount of money paid in addition to regular wages or salaries.

business entity [N-COUNT-U2] A **business entity** is any type of business.

buy out [V-PHRASE-U4] To **buy out** a business is to purchase it at a time when it is about to go out of business.

campaign [N-COUNT-U11] A **campaign** is an organized, planned set of actions.

carry over [V-PHRASE-U9] To **carry over** something is to transfer it from one period to another.

cash basis accounting [N-UNCOUNT-U8] **Cash basis accounting** is an accounting method that involves recording only the exchange of cash.

cash collections [N-UNCOUNT-U1] **Cash collections** are activities in which someone receives money that is owed to a company.

cash disbursements [N-COUNT-U1] **Cash disbursements** are activities in which a company pays money that it owes.

catch (someone's) attention [V-PHRASE-U12] To **catch someone's attention** is to cause him or her to notice something.

charitable [ADJ-U11] If something is **charitable**, it is done to help other people, rather than to make a profit.

checking account [N-COUNT-U1] A **checking account** is a bank account from which payments are made.

chief financial officer [N-COUNT-U3] A **chief financial officer** is an executive who is the highest authority over an organization's financial activities.

collateral [N-UNCOUNT-U10] **Collateral** is an asset used as security against a loan.

competitive intangible [N-COUNT-U5] A **competitive intangible** is a non-physical valuable that is not protected by law, such as reputation or popularity.

condemn [V-T-U15] To **condemn** something is to judge it as being wrong.

conservatism [N-UNCOUNT-U2] **Conservatism** is an idea and practice that avoids risks and major changes.

controller [N-COUNT-U3] A **controller** is a person who oversees all of an organization's financial activities.

copyright [N-COUNT-U5] A **copyright** is a legal protection of written material.

corporation [N-COUNT-U2] A **corporation** is a business that is legally recognized as a single unit.

criticize [V-T-U15] To **criticize** someone is to state objections to that person's behavior.

damages [N-UNCOUNT-U14] **Damages** (usually plural) are fines that a losing party in a lawsuit is required to pay to the winning party.

data mining [N-UNCOUNT-U13] **Data mining** is the analysis of information to find patterns within it.

deceit [N-UNCOUNT-U7] **Deceit** is the act of lying or intentionally misleading.

default [V-I-U10] To **default** is to fail to make payments.

desirable terms [ADJ+N-COUNT-U10] **Desirable terms** are loan conditions that are favorable.

discontinue [V-T-U11] To **discontinue** something is to stop it.

discontinuity [N-COUNT-U14] A **discontinuity** is an item that does not conform to the accepted normal pattern.

downsize [V-I-U14] To **downsize** is to reduce the overall dimensions of a business.

drug screening [N-COUNT-U3] A **drug screening** is a test performed to see if there are illegal drugs in a person's body.

earnings before interest and tax (EBIT) [N-UNCOUNT-U5] **Earnings before interest and tax (EBIT)** is the money that remains after fixed and variable expenses have been deducted.

ease of use [N-UNCOUNT-U13] **Ease of use** is the degree to which something is simple and easy to use.

embezzle [V-T-U7] To **embezzle** resources is to take them from an organization and use them for oneself.

employee benefit [N-COUNT-U11] An **employee benefit** is any form of compensation other than wages and salaries.

environmentally friendly [ADJ-U15] If something is **environmentally friendly**, it does not cause pollution or other environmental degradation.

ethical [ADJ-U15] If something is **ethical**, it adheres to accepted standards of appropriate behavior.

excessive [ADJ-U4] If something is **excessive** it is more than what is needed.

expenditure [N-COUNT-U4] An **expenditure** is an instance of spending money.

Glossary

exploit [V-T-U15] To **exploit** someone is to use him or her unfairly.

external financial report [N-COUNT-U3] An **external financial report** is a document prepared for and used by people outside of an organization.

extraordinary [ADJ-U14] If something is **extraordinary**, it is beyond what is considered normal.

falsification [N-UNCOUNT-U7] **Falsification** is the act of deliberately putting false information into records.

fixed expense [N-COUNT-U6] A **fixed expense** is one that stays the same each month.

flow of transactions [N-UNCOUNT-U12] A **flow of transactions** is the pattern of buying and selling that a business goes through.

forgery [N-UNCOUNT-U7] A **forgery** is an illegal copy of something.

fraud [N-UNCOUNT-U7] **Fraud** is the act of cheating someone out of money or other resources.

full disclosure [N-UNCOUNT-U2] **Full disclosure** is the act of revealing all available information.

functionality [N-UNCOUNT-U13] **Functionality** is the degree to which something is practical and useful.

garbage in, garbage out [PHRASE-U13] **Garbage in, garbage out** means that flawed inputs will result in flawed outputs.

goodwill [N-UNCOUNT-U5] **Goodwill** is the value that a company derives from its reputation and popularity.

gross earnings [N-UNCOUNT-U1] **Gross earnings** are the total amount of money before deductions that an employee earns.

gross wages [N-UNCOUNT-U1] **Gross wages** are the sum of an employee's hourly pay for a certain period.

hold (someone) accountable [V-PHRASE-U7] To **hold someone accountable** is to require that the person take responsibility for his or her actions.

immoral [ADJ-U15] If something is **immoral**, it does not adhere to accepted standards of appropriate behavior.

impaired [ADJ-U14] If something is **impaired**, it is not able to fulfill its desired function.

income tax payable [N-UNCOUNT-U9] **Income tax payable** is the amount of tax that an organization owes a government for a certain year but is not required to pay until the following year.

increment [N-COUNT-U8] An **increment** is one of a certain number of sections that something has been divided into.

insufficient [ADJ-U4] If something is **insufficient** it is less than what is needed.

intangible asset [N-COUNT-U5] An **intangible asset** is anything of value that is not a physical object.

integrity [N-UNCOUNT-U3] **Integrity** is a characteristic involving adherence to moral and professional standards.

interest rate [N-COUNT-U10] An **interest rate** is a percentage that is added to a loan amount during the loan period.

internal financial report [N-COUNT-U3] An **internal financial report** is a document prepared for and used by members of an organization.

kick-back [N-COUNT-U7] A **kick-back** is a bribe paid in exchange for favorable treatment.

lawsuit [N-COUNT-U14] A **lawsuit** is a formal legal proceeding.

layoff [V-T-U14] To **layoff** someone is to stop employing them because the company cannot offer them anymore work, for example due to recession.

legal intangible [N-COUNT-U5] A **legal intangible** is a non-physical valuable that is protected by law.

level off [V-PHRASE-U11] To **level off** is to stop rising or falling.

leverage [V-T-U10] To **leverage** something is to use it as collateral to get a loan.

liquidity [N-UNCOUNT-U4] **Liquidity** is the degree of ease with which an asset can be converted to cash.

loan period [N-COUNT-U9] A **loan period** is the amount of time in which a debt is expected to be paid.

low road [N-UNCOUNT-U15] The **low road** is any course of action that is immoral.

make a killing [V-PHRASE-U15] To **make a killing** is to make a huge amount of profit.

margin per unit [N-UNCOUNT-U6] **Margin per unit** is the revenue left over after variable expenses divided by the number of units produced.

misappropriate [V-T-U7] To **misappropriate** something is to distribute it to the wrong recipient.

most-likely scenario [N-UNCOUNT-U2] The **most-likely scenario** is the situation that has the most chance of happening.

objectivity [N-UNCOUNT-U2] **Objectivity** is the practice of not allowing feelings or opinions to influence judgment.

on credit [ADV-U8] To purchase something **on credit** is to purchase it with a promise to pay for it later.

operating earnings [N-UNCOUNT-U6] **Operating earnings** is the money left after fixed and variable expenses have been deducted.

optimistic [ADJ-U2] If someone is **optimistic**, it means that he or she sees future events positively.

origination fee [N-COUNT-U10] An **origination fee** is an amount of money that a creditor charges for creating a loan.

out of the ordinary [ADJ-U12] If something is **out of the ordinary**, it is not normal.

partnership [N-COUNT-U2] A **partnership** is an unincorporated business that is owned by a few people.

patent right [N-COUNT-U5] A **patent right** is a legal protection of an invention.

pay for (something) ahead of time [V-PHRASE-U8] To **pay for something ahead of time** is to pay for it before receiving it.

pay off [V-T-U10] To **pay off** a loan is to repay the total amount of it plus any interest.

pay stub [N-COUNT-U1] A **pay stub** is a document that shows an employees pay and taxes for a certain period.

pilfer [V-T-U7] To **pilfer** something is to steal it from one's employer.

poverty line [N-UNCOUNT-U15] The **poverty line** is the amount of money that a person needs to cover basic needs.

prepaid expense asset [N-COUNT-U8] A **prepaid expense asset** is the recorded amount of an advance payment.

procurement [N-COUNT-U1] **Procurement** is the act of obtaining things.

profit center [N-COUNT-U6] A **profit center** is a division within a company that generates money.

Glossary

profit sharing plan [N-COUNT-U11] A **profit sharing plan** is a project in which a company gives a portion of its income to its employees.

purchase order [N-COUNT-U1] A **purchase order** is a document stating items that a company wishes to buy.

receipt [N-COUNT-U4] A **receipt** is something that is received.

red flag [N-COUNT-U12] A **red flag** is a detail that is alarming.

relevance [N-UNCOUNT-U2] **Relevance** is the state of being important and practically applicable.

remote access [N-UNCOUNT-U13] **Remote access** is the ability to use a program from a computer or electronic device other than the one that the program is installed on.

repairs [N-UNCOUNT-U11] **Repairs** are the activities involved with fixing something that is broken.

restructure [V-I-U14] To **restructure** is to change the basic composition of a company.

retailer [N-COUNT-U6] A **retailer** is a company that sells products to the public.

safety reserve [N-COUNT-U4] A **safety reserve** is an amount that is held in case of unforeseen needs.

salary [N-COUNT-U1] A **salary** is a yearly amount of money paid to an employee.

sales volume [N-UNCOUNT-U6] **Sales volume** is the total number of products sold.

senior claim [N-UNCOUNT-U10] A **senior claim** is the right to draw on a debtor's assets.

severance package [N-COUNT-U14] A **severance package** is an amount of money and/or other benefits given to an employee when he or she is fired.

shoplift [V-T-U7] To **shoplift** is to steal something from a retail store.

sole proprietorship [N-COUNT-U2] A **sole proprietorship** is a business that is owned by just one person.

spike [N-COUNT-U11] A **spike** is a sharp increase.

stiff [V-T-U12] To **stiff** someone is to fail to pay him or her for goods or services.

sweep [N-COUNT-U12] A **sweep** is a quick scan of something.

take out [V-PHRASE-U10] To **take out** a loan is to borrow money.

tangible asset [N-COUNT-U5] A **tangible asset** is any physical object that holds value.

tax deductible [ADJ-U10] If something is **tax deductible**, its value can be subtracted from its owner's taxable income.

temporary [ADJ-U11] If something is **temporary**, it has a limited duration.

total margin [N-UNCOUNT-U6] **Total margin** is the revenue left over after variable expenses have been deducted.

total wages [N-UNCOUNT-U1] **Total wages** are the sum of an employee's hourly pay for a certain period.

trade secret [N-COUNT-U5] A **trade secret** is crucial knowledge like a recipe or manufacturing technique.

trademark [N-COUNT-U5] A **trademark** is a legally protected symbol.

tutorial [N-COUNT-U13] A **tutorial** is a document or program that teaches someone how to do something.

unbiased [ADJ-U1] If someone is **unbiased**, he or she practices objectivity.

unethical [ADJ-U15] If something is **unethical**, it does not adhere to accepted standards of appropriate behavior.

unproductive [ADJ-U4] If something is **unproductive** it is not growing or having any positive change.

up and running [ADJ-U13] If something is **up and running**, it is now fully operational.

up to date [ADJ-U3] If something is **up to date**, it means that it includes all available information as of today.

update [N-COUNT-U13] An **update** is an improvement for a program.

user license [N-COUNT-U13] A **user license** is the official legal permission to use a computer program.

user-friendly [ADJ-U13] If something is **user-friendly**, it is easy to use.

variable expense [N-COUNT-U6] A **variable expense** is one that is likely to change each month.

via [PREP-U9] **Via** means that something takes place or is done through something else.

wholesaler [N-COUNT-U6] A **wholesaler** is a company that sells products to retailers.

zero cash balance [N-UNCOUNT-U4] A **zero cash balance** is a situation in which there is no cash in an account.

Book 3

John Taylor
Stephen Peltier - C.P.A., M.S.

Express Publishing

Scope and Sequence

Unit	Topic	Reading context	Vocabulary	Function
1	The Language of Accounting	Magazine Article	combined, convention, custom, double underline, general and administrative costs, insurance premium, jargon, minus sign, second-nature, utility	Giving reasons
2	Analyzing Balance Sheets	Magazine Article	creditor, debt-to-equity ratio, fundamental analysis, growth potential, security valuation, side-by-side comparison, statement of financial condition, working capital	Asking about difficulty
3	Fraud	Magazine Article	administrative leave, bribery, cook the books, juggle the accounts, make false entries, money-laundering, reroute, sales skimming, under-the-table	Expressing disbelief
4	Solvency	Emails	barring, catastrophe, current ratio, indicator, involuntary bankruptcy, operating cycle, repetitive, solvency, think twice, unforeseen	Asking for advice
5	Direct and Indirect Costs	Textbook	activity-based costing, cost driver, direct cost, direct labor, direct materials, fixed cost, fixed overhead, indirect cost, variable cost, variable overhead	Asking for instructions
6	Budgeting	Textbook	business budgeting, concrete goal, educated guess, forecast, long-term, model, near-term, negative outlook, positive outlook, short-term, tighten, yardstick	Discussing possible events
7	Auditing	Letter	anomalous, capitalized, clean opinion, clerical error, COO, cutoff point, erroneous, impropriety, material adjustment, professional skepticism	Checking for certainty
8	The Break-even Point	Email	break-even point, delicate, lock in, loss zone, margin ratio, optimal, profit zone, recoup, slump	Listing options
9	Globalization	Journal Article	adopt, apply globally, free circulation, globalized standard, IASC, inevitable, mid-size, strategic decision, worldwide trend	Talking about changes
10	Communicating with Clients	Blog	body language, convenience, instant clarification, linguistic cue, non-verbal cue, reflection, slang, stay in touch, tonal cue, verbal cue, vernacular	Asking about problems
11	Viability	Emails	advisory, astronomical, buyout, cost effective, local knowledge, plant, raise capital, supply and distribution channel, venture, viability	Giving an honest opinion
12	Buy or Lease?	Magazine Article	down-payment, early termination, economic value, finance, financier, lease, lease term, lease, lessee, lessor, run the numbers, useful life	Acknowledging a problem
13	Tax Havens	Advertisement	business association, flat tax, impose, levy, progressive taxation, promote, tax avoidance, tax bracket, tax break, tax evasion	Expressing doubts
14	Tax Accounting	Promotional Literature	board of accountancy, evaluate, expertise, in-house, outsource, privacy policy, quality assurance, review process, tedious, third party	Providing reassurance
15	The Future of Accounting	Journal Article	acquisition, attest service, audit opinion, electronic commerce, flex location, flextime, litigation support, merger, public practice, risk assessment, service-based economy	Describing new opportunities

Table of Contents

Unit 1 – The Language of Accounting 4

Unit 2 – Analyzing Balance Sheets 6

Unit 3 – Fraud 8

Unit 4 – Solvency 10

Unit 5 – Direct and Indirect Costs 12

Unit 6 – Budgeting 14

Unit 7 – Auditing 16

Unit 8 – The Break-even Point 18

Unit 9 – Globalization 20

Unit 10 – Communicating with Clients 22

Unit 11 – Viability 24

Unit 12 – Buy or Lease? 26

Unit 13 – Tax Havens 28

Unit 14 – Tax Accounting 30

Unit 15 – The Future of Accounting 32

Glossary 34

1 The Language of Accounting

Accounting and Finance – October, 2011 – Page 65

Get ready!

1 Before you read the passage, talk about these questions.

1. How can income statements, like below, cause confusion to non-accountants?
2. How can accounting terms cause confusion?

Income Statement
Year ended December 31

Sales Revenue	$1,000,000
Cost of Goods Sold	($700,000)
Gross Margin	$300,000
Operating Costs	($150,000)
Margin	$150,000
Fixed Expenses	($60,000)
Earnings	**$90,000**

Ask the CPA!

— by Chuck Daley

This week, I'd like to address a very common problem. There is often a major communication breakdown between accountants and non-accountants. We bean-counters mistakenly assume that everyone understands our **jargon** and the **conventions** of financial reporting. We are so wrong.

I'm going to point out five of the most common financial reporting **customs** that are **second-nature** to accountants but often misunderstood by non-accountants:

1. There are no **minus signs** on most financial reports. When a number is meant to be subtracted it is often indicated by putting it in parentheses.
2. The bottom line is presented in an eye-catching way. Accountants will often use a **double underline** or bold text in the bottom line.
3. The word "profit" is rarely used. Instead, accountants usually use "net income" or "earnings."
4. Revenue is reported as the **combined** total of all sales during a particular period. Details about that sales revenue are not reported.
5. Similar to revenue, operating costs are reported in a lump sum rather than individual values. This includes selling, **general and administrative costs**, **insurance premiums**, **utilities**, etc.

It's good to learn these customs. When in doubt, just ask your accountants. Remember, it's part of their job to help you understand your business's finances.

Reading

2 Read this article from a business magazine. Then, choose the correct answers.

1. What is the passage mainly about?
   - A why accountants should not use certain kinds of jargon
   - B how to avoid mathematical errors in financial reports
   - C how accounting conventions confuse non-accountants
   - D when to suggest changes to financial reporting customs

2. All sources of sales revenue are reported as
   - A profits.
   - B a combined total.
   - C operational costs.
   - D individual values.

3. How are negative numbers indicated on income statements?
   - A with parentheses
   - B with a minus sign
   - C with a single underline
   - D with a double underline

Vocabulary

3 Match the words or phrases (1-5) with the definitions (A-E).

1. __ jargon
2. __ conventions
3. __ general and administrative costs
4. __ insurance premium
5. __ utilities

- A a fee that is paid for financial protection
- B the amounts paid for basic business operations
- C generally accepted patterns of behavior
- D conveniences like water, gas, and electricity
- E language that is unique to a certain group

4 Fill in the blanks with the correct words or phrases from the word bank.

Word BANK

customs   second-nature
double underline   combine   minus sign

1 Lydia made so many reports that it became _____ .
2 Show final amounts, like earnings, with a _____ .
3 Jack is learning the _____ of financial reporting.
4 Don't show the amounts separately; _____ them.
5 Accountants use parentheses instead of a _____ .

5 🎧 Listen and read the article again. What words/expressions do accountants use instead of profit?

Listening

6 🎧 Listen to a conversation between an accountant and a manager. Mark the following statements as true (T) or false (F).

1 __ The report showed several types of revenue.
2 __ The report was in a different language.
3 __ Accountants may sometimes use the term "profit."

7 🎧 Listen again and complete the conversation.

Manager:	Hello, Lillian. Can I talk to you about our financial reports?
Accountant:	OK. Was there a problem?
Manager:	No, I'm just having trouble understanding some parts of them.
Accountant:	Oh, I know what you mean. We accountants kind of have our own language.
Manager:	Could you explain to me how you set up this income statement.
Accountant:	Absolutely. **1** _____ _____ _____ no minus signs?
Manager:	Yes. That's one of the **2** _____ _____ _____ me.
Accountant:	Well, I've **3** _____ _____ _____ where we subtract by putting the number in parentheses.
Manager:	Oh, I see that now.
Accountant:	OK, so, another thing you might have noticed is that we don't give a lot of details on the entries.
Manager:	Is that why I **4** _____ _____ _____ _____ for sales revenue?
Accountant:	Exactly. We **5** _____ _____ _____ _____ into direct sales, retail sales, etc. We just **6** _____ _____ _____ of all sales.
Manager:	OK. That makes sense. But, you know, I don't see profit anywhere on this report.

Speaking

8 With a partner, act out the roles below based on Task 7. Then switch roles.

USE LANGUAGE SUCH AS:
I'm just having trouble understanding ...
I know what you mean.
You notice there are ...?

Student A: You are a manager. Talk to Student B about:
- confusion about financial reports
- symbols used on reports
- terms used on reports

Student B: You are an accountant. Answer Student A's questions.

Writing

9 You are an accountant. Use the article and the conversation from Task 8, write a brief memo to non-accountants in your company about accounting language. Talk about:

- Financial reports
- Symbols that you use
- Terms that you use
- Items that are included/excluded

memo
From:
To:
Subject:

2 Analyzing Balance Sheets

What's the Deal with the Balance Sheet?

Business Edition – Spring Issue – Page 50

by Ben Chapman

You see them all the time. Accountants at your firm produce these nice little statements called balance sheets. What useful information can this document tell you?

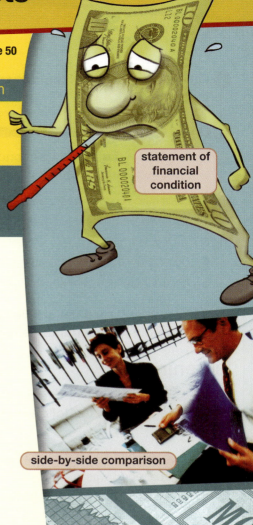

statement of financial condition

side-by-side comparison

security valuation

The balance sheet is like a snapshot of a company's financial situation at a moment in time. That's why it is sometimes called a "**statement of financial condition**." It shows a **side-by-side comparison** of a company's assets and its liabilities and equity. Assets include things like cash, accounts receivable, and equipment. Liabilities include things like accounts payable and debts owed to **creditors**.

The balance sheet is one of the basic tools in **fundamental analysis**. Fundamental analysis helps to determine **security valuation** as well as **growth potential**. A major factor that you will want to analyze is your company's **working capital**, which is current assets minus current liabilities.

Additionally, you will want to calculate your debt-to-equity ratio. This is simply a comparison of total liabilities to owner's equity. To find it, divide total liabilities by owner's equity. The resulting ratio indicates how much of your company's operations are funded by debt compared to equity. For example, a **debt-to-equity ratio** of two means that your company is run with twice as much borrowed money as equity. •••

Get ready!

1 Before you read the passage, talk about these questions.

1 What things are included in balance sheets?
2 What do balance sheets tell us about companies?

Reading

2 Read this magazine article. Then mark the following statements as true (T) or false (F).

1 __ A statement of financial condition shows debt.
2 __ Determine working capital by subtracting current liabilities from current assets.
3 __ Liabilities minus equity equals debt-to-equity ratio.

Vocabulary

3 Match the words or phrases (1-4) with the definitions (A-D).

1 __ working capital   3 __ fundamental analysis
2 __ creditors   4 __ debt-to-equity ratio

A a comparison of what a company owes to what it is worth
B people or companies that are owed money
C assets minus liabilities
D an examination of value and growth potential

4 Fill in the blanks with the correct words or phrases: *security valuation*, *side-by-side comparison*, *growth potential*, *statement of financial condition*.

1 _____ is the ability of a company to expand.
2 A _____ is also called a balance sheet.
3 Paul performed a _____ of revenue and expenses.
4 Stock prices are set after _____ .

5 Listen and read the article again. What items are included in a liabilities figure on a balance sheet?

Listening

6 Listen to a conversation between an accountant and a manager. Choose the correct answers.

1 What are the people talking about?
- A the need to purchase assets
- B a plan to borrow some money
- C why their working capital is rising
- D the company's unusually high debt

2 What does the woman suggest?
- A liquidating assets
- B taking out a loan
- C laying off employees
- D collecting from debtors

7 Listen again and complete the conversation.

Manager:	Hello, Karen. Could I talk to you about those reports that you submitted last week?
Accountant:	Sure. Is there a problem?
Manager:	Well, I'm not sure. A couple things caught my eye, but I'm not sure how to interpret them.
Accountant:	OK. I'll see if I can help.
Manager:	Great. On the balance sheet, I noticed that our debt is almost twice what it was last period.
Accountant:	Right. That's because we took a short term loan to cover some unexpected expenses.
Manager:	Oh, that's right. Still, I'm a little worried about it.
Accountant:	Are you thinking we should **1** _____ _____ _____ ?
Manager:	Maybe. Do you think we'll **2** _____ _____ _____ _____ those debts?
Accountant:	Let's see ... we can calculate our working capital. **3** _____ _____ _____ a good idea.
Manager:	OK. Is that a **4** _____ _____ ?
Accountant:	Not at all. Just subtract current liabilities from current assets.
Manager:	Oh, I see. That makes sense.
Accountant:	It looks like our assets are still **5** _____ _____ _____ our liabilities.
Manager:	Great. That **6** _____ _____ _____ _____ . How should we start paying off our debt?
Accountant:	We should try to collect our accounts receivable and use those funds to pay our debts.

Speaking

8 With a partner, act out the roles below based on Task 7. Then switch roles.

> **USE LANGUAGE SUCH AS:**
> *I noticed that ...*
> *Are you thinking ...?*
> *How should we start paying off our debt?*

Student A: You are a manager. Talk to Student B about:
- unusually high debt
- working capital
- ways to reduce debt

Student B: You are an accountant. Answer Student A's questions.

Writing

9 You are an accountant. Use the article and the conversation from Task 8 to write a brief email to your manager. Talk about:

- unusually high debt
- where the debt came from
- working capital
- options for reducing debt

3 Fraud

The many faces of fraud

Legal Weekly – April 17 – Page 32

by Tina Maxwell

An accountant at a school in the United States recently pled guilty to embezzlement charges. The accountant **rerouted** hundreds of thousands of dollars from school accounts to her personal accounts. How did she do it? Simple. Over a period of three years, she wrote numerous checks to herself and gave herself unauthorized raises. She concealed her activities by **making false entries** such as payments to vendors and other companies. Eventually, her employer found out and she was placed on **administrative leave**. Incredibly, she continued to write herself company checks, even though she was no longer working for them. This accountant's story of **cooking the books** is all too common. Fraud is a widespread phenomenon.

Fraud occurs in all types of businesses — big and small. Some crimes, like **sales skimming**, are more common in small businesses while other crimes, like **money-laundering**, happen more often in large businesses. Theft is not always the motive of fraud. Sometimes, individuals or companies seek to enhance their economic or political position through **bribery**. They may accept kickbacks or **under-the-table payoffs** from suppliers. Or they might bribe a public official to represent their political interests. Whatever the methods or motives, **juggling the accounts** is a serious crime, and carries severe penalties.

…

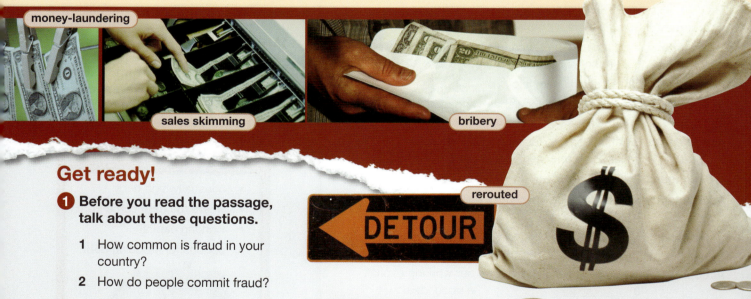

Get ready!

1 Before you read the passage, talk about these questions.

1 How common is fraud in your country?
2 How do people commit fraud?

Reading

2 Read this magazine article. Then, mark the following statements as true (T) or false (F).

1 __ Money laundering is a type of embezzlement.
2 __ People can hide illegal activity by making false entries.
3 __ Sales skimming is not common in large businesses.

Vocabulary

3 Match the words or phrases (1-5) with the definitions (A-E).

1 __ reroute
2 __ bribery
3 __ money-laundering
4 __ making false entries
5 __ sales skimming

A illegally directing money through a corporation
B the act of paying for favorable treatment
C to direct something to a different destination
D the act of recording erroneous amounts
E taking revenue from one's employer

4 Read the sentence pairs. Choose which word or phrase best fits each blank.

1 administrative leave / cooking the books
   A The numbers are wrong. Someone is _____.
   B Sharon was placed on _____ for rerouting funds.

2 under-the-table payoffs / juggling the accounts
   A The manager took _____ from a supplier.
   B An accountant was _____ to hide sales skimming.

5 🎧 Listen and read the article again. What happens to those who are caught committing fraud?

Listening

6 🎧 Listen to a conversation between two accountants. Choose the correct answers.

1 What is the dialogue mostly about?
   A criminal charges   C business expenses
   B suspicious entries   D bookkeeping errors

2 What did Mr. Donaldson do?
   A He embezzled company funds.
   B He went on a business trip.
   C He bribed an official.
   D He made false expense entries.

7 🎧 Listen again and complete the conversation.

Accountant 1:	Amusement park tickets? Seriously? How can you **1** _____ that as a business expense?
Accountant 2:	You can't. And didn't he say something about going to an amusement park **2** _____ ?
Accountant 1:	He did. He's obviously using the business to **3** _____ expenses.
Accountant 2:	And he's just **4** _____ _____ . You know what they say – pigs get fat; hogs get slaughtered.
Accountant 1:	That's right. So did you find any entries **5** _____ _____ ?
Accountant 2:	Well, there was this one for office supplies.
Accountant 1:	So what? Every business buys office supplies.
Accountant 2:	Yeah, but this entry was **6** _____ bigger than all the past office supply purchases.
Accountant 1:	Whoa. So either he's buying a few years' worth of office supplies, or ...
Accountant 2:	Or he's making a false entry to cover something up.

Speaking

8 With a partner, act out the roles below based on Task 7. Then switch roles.

USE LANGUAGE SUCH AS:

Seriously?
How can you possibly ...?
He's obviously using ...
Did you find any entries ...?

Student A: You are an accountant. Talk to Student B about:
• suspicious entries in a client's books
• the possibility of fraud

Student B: You are an accountant. Answer Student A's questions.

Writing

9 You are an accountant. Use the article and the conversation from Task 8 to write a brief letter to your manager. Talk about:

• reviewing a client's books
• personal expenses in business books
• unusually large entries
• the possibility of fraud

4 Solvency

From: Vanessa Moore, Manager
To: Hank Bally, Controller

Good morning, Hank. I'd really like to get your opinion on something. We're thinking about investing in an outside company. I want to make sure that we choose the right one. I've read too many stories lately about corporations being forced into **involuntary bankruptcy** because of their inability to pay creditors. So, my question for you is, how can I determine a company's **solvency**?

From: Hank Bally, Controller
To: Vanessa Moore, Manager

Hi, Vanessa. Unfortunately, solvency cannot be predicted with 100% accuracy. But **barring** any **unforeseen catastrophes**, you can get a good idea of a company's solvency by analyzing its **operating cycle** — the **repetitive** pattern of producing goods or services and selling them for profit. Within that cycle, you should calculate the company's **current ratio**. Let me explain what this number is.

The current ratio is an **indicator** of a company's ability to pay its liabilities. To calculate current ratio, just divide the company's current assets by its current liabilities. For example, if its current assets total $400,000 and its current liabilities total $160,000, then its current ratio is 2.5. That's an excellent ratio indicating strong solvency. Generally speaking, a ratio of 2.0 or above is considered good. With anything under 2.0, **think twice**.

Get ready!

1 Before you read the passage, talk about these questions.

1. What is solvency?
2. How can solvency be predicted?

Reading

2 Read these emails. Then, mark the following statements as true (T) or false (F).

1. ___ A current ratio predicts future income.
2. ___ Operating cycles can demonstrate solvency.
3. ___ A current ratio under 2.0 is considered good.

Vocabulary

3 Match the words or phrases (1-5) with the definitions (A-E).

1. ___ solvency
2. ___ barring
3. ___ involuntary bankruptcy
4. ___ unforeseen
5. ___ think twice

A a situation in which a business runs out of money
B a business's ability to pay its expenses
C not including
D not able to be predicted
E to consider something carefully

4 Fill in the blanks with the correct words or phrases:
indicator, current ratio, catastrophe, repetitive, operating cycle.

1. Monthly sales patterns are _____ .
2. A(n) _____ is a pattern of buying and selling.
3. The _____ shows a company's solvency.
4. Economic depression can be quite a _____ .
5. Sales may not be a(n) _____ of a company's health.

5 🎧 Listen and read the emails again. How can an investor be reasonably sure that a company won't go bankrupt?

Listening

6 🎧 Listen to a conversation between two accountants. Choose the correct answers.

1. What is the dialogue mostly about?
   A a recent investment
   B a company's solvency
   C decreasing a current ratio
   D strengthening a company's financials

2. What is the woman likely to do?
   A fire her controller
   B invest in Essential Products
   C look for another investment
   D ask for another accountant's opinion

7 🎧 Listen again and complete the conversation.

Manager:	Well, it's a manufacturing company called Essential Products Manufacturing.
Controller:	OK. How do its numbers look?
Manager:	Um, well, I calculated its current ratio with that formula you sent me. It was one point four five.
Controller:	Hmm ... **1** _____ _____ . It's pretty low.
Manager:	Really? Another accountant told me it's **2** _____ _____ _____ if the current ratio is below two.
Controller:	Well, **3** _____ _____ _____ it's not. But just remember, the ratio shows the **4** _____ _____ to pay its debts.
Manager:	So, **5** _____ _____ _____ _____ , the more risk of not paying debts and going bankrupt?
Controller:	Yes, exactly. A higher ratio means a stronger, more stable company.
Manager:	So, what do you think I should do?
Controller:	I think you should **6** _____ _____ _____ a different company.

Speaking

8 With a partner, act out the roles below based on Task 7. Then switch roles.

USE LANGUAGE SUCH AS:

Can I get your opinion on a specific company?

How do its numbers look?

The lower the number ...

Student A: You are a manager. Talk to Student B about:
- a company to invest in
- the company's current ratio
- the company's solvency

Student B: You are a controller. Answer Student A's questions.

Writing

9 You are a controller. Your manager asked for your opinion about investing in a company. Use the emails and the conversation from Task 8 to write a brief email answering your manager's questions. Talk about:
- the company's current ratio
- the company's solvency
- your recommendation

5 Direct and Indirect Costs

Accounting for Costs

Some costs are easy to account for. **Direct costs**, which are also called **variable costs**, are easily attributed to a specific product or activity. For example, a company that makes pens has to buy plastic and ink and pay its employees to manufacture the pens. These are obviously direct costs. But businesses also incur **indirect costs,** or **fixed costs**, which remain constant and are not tied to specific products or services. Take, for example, a manufacturing company.

Manufacturing firms have both direct and indirect costs.

Direct costs include:
- Raw materials, often called **direct materials**
- **Direct labor** – the wages paid to production-line employees
- **Variable overhead** – other costs that increase or decrease with production (For example, if production requires water, the water bill will fluctuate with the volume of production.)

Indirect manufacturing costs include:
- **Fixed overhead** – depreciation, insurance, rents

So how should indirect costs be accounted for? One popular method is called **activity-based costing (ABC)**. In this method, cost drivers are created for each product. Then indirect costs are allocated according to those **cost drivers**. For example, in a manufacturing plant, an indirect cost like rent could be allocated to each piece of machinery based on how much space it occupies.

Get ready!

1 Before you read the passage, talk about these questions.
1. What are direct costs?
2. What are indirect costs?

Reading

2 Read this article in an accounting textbook. Then, mark the following statements as true (T) or false (F).

1. __ The ABC method can account for fixed costs.
2. __ Variable overhead is directly tied to production.
3. __ Cost drivers are used to allocate direct costs.

Vocabulary

3 Match the phrases (1-5) with the definitions (A-E).

1. __ variable cost
2. __ direct labor
3. __ activity-based costing
4. __ indirect cost
5. __ cost drivers

A any expense tied to production
B any expense not tied to production
C units involved in production
D the cost of paying workers
E a method for allocating fixed costs

4 Choose the sentence that uses the underlined part correctly.

1. A Rent is an example of <u>fixed overhead</u>.
   B A loan payment is <u>variable overhead</u>.
2. A <u>Direct materials</u> are used to make products.
   B An insurance premium is a <u>direct cost</u>.
3. A <u>Variable overhead</u> is not tied to production.
   B A <u>fixed cost</u> is not tied to production.
4. A An employee's wage is a <u>direct cost</u>.
   B An executive's bonus is <u>fixed overhead</u>.
5. A The price of paint is a <u>fixed cost</u>.
   B <u>Variable overhead</u> is costs tied to production.

5 🎧 **Listen and read the article again. How might you account for a cost like rent in a manufacturing company?**

Listening

6 🎧 **Listen to a conversation between two accountants. Choose the correct answers.**

1 What is the dialogue mostly about?
  A allocating direct costs
  B renting versus owning
  C pairing costs with prices
  D direct versus indirect costs

2 The cost of metal is
  A a cost driver.
  B a variable cost.
  C fixed overhead.
  D an indirect cost.

7 🎧 **Listen again and complete the conversation.**

Client: Hi, Sarah. Thanks for helping me set up my books.
Accountant: No problem. That's what I'm here for. Let's start by listing your direct and indirect costs.
Client: Direct and indirect costs? I'm sorry ... I'm not sure I understand.
Accountant: Well, direct costs are tied directly to a product or service.
Client: OK. Can you give me an example?
Accountant: Um, your company makes paper clips, right? The cost of the metal is a direct cost.
Client: So, then, what would be an indirect cost?
Accountant: Let's see ... do you own your manufacturing plant?
Client: No, I rent it.
Accountant: Well, your rent 1 _____ _____ _____ _____ how many paper clips you manufacture. It's an indirect cost.
Client: Oh, I see. So, how 2 _____ _____ _____ _____ these different types of costs?
Accountant: It's easy with the direct costs. 3 _____ _____ _____ _____ the money that you get from selling your products.
Client: Right. But what about the indirect costs? 4 _____ _____ _____ there's a method called ABC. What is that?
Accountant: It's a way to allocate indirect costs 5 _____ _____ _____ .
Client: Can you show me how to do that?
Accountant: Well, 6 _____ _____ _____ . Let me explain ...

Speaking

8 **With a partner, act out the roles below based on Task 7. Then switch roles.**

USE LANGUAGE SUCH AS:
What would be ...?
Do you own ...?
How should I ...?

Student A: You are a business owner. Talk to Student B about:
- indirect costs
- how to record different types of costs

Student B: You are an accountant. Answer Student A's questions.

Writing

9 **You are an accountant. Use the article and the conversation from Task 8 to write a brief email to your client explaining different types of costs. Talk about:**

- direct/variable costs
- indirect/fixed costs
- how to record costs
- the ABC (activity-based costing) method

6 Budgeting

Get ready!

1 Before you read the passage, talk about these questions.

1. Why does a business need to make a budget?
2. How do businesses use their budgets?

Reading

2 Read this passage from a textbook. Then, mark the following statements as true (T) or false (F).

1. __ Businesses use budgets to measure their progress.
2. __ Forecasts determine outlook.
3. __ Budgets are tighter when the economic outlook is gloomy.

Vocabulary

3 Match the words or phrases (1-6) with the definitions (A-F).

1. __ forecast
2. __ tighten
3. __ near-term
4. __ long-term
5. __ yardstick
6. __ negative outlook

A. a tool used to measure something
B. to reduce activity and flexibility
C. over a lengthy period of time
D. a gloomy view of the future
E. a prediction about the future
F. over a small period of time

Why Budget?

Imagine wanting to build a house. Would you carefully draw up detailed plans that showed every part of the structure that you wanted to build? Or would you gather a hammer, some nails, and some pieces of wood and just start putting everything together? It makes no sense to build something without a plan. This principle is true in the business world as well.

No one would try to run a business without a plan. A great way to plan for the financial future is **business budgeting**. Businesses budget by setting **concrete goals** built on realistic **forecasts**. Obviously, it costs time and money to develop such detailed **models**. Managers must make **educated guesses** about how much they can invest in budgeting. They must also decide whether to budget **long-term** or **short-term** (also called **near-term**).

Despite the cost, budgeting is an essential business function. It serves as a **yardstick** for measuring the company's performance. In other words, it can compare its goals to its accomplishments at the end of a budget period. Budgeting also serves as a blueprint for the future. If a forecast predicts economic decline, a company will **tighten** its budget. But if this **negative outlook** is reversed and economic expansion is predicted, the budget may be expanded to reflect a more **positive outlook**.

positive outlook

forecast

negative outlook

4 Fill in the blanks with the correct words or phrases from the word bank.

Word BANK

concrete goals   business budgeting
model   short-term   positive outlook

1. Set _____ and then pursue them.
2. Companies have a(n) _____ when the economy looks good.
3. _____ is one of the best ways to plan ahead.
4. The budget is _____ , covering just two months.
5. A budget is a _____ based on plans and forecasts.

5 🎧 Listen and read the passage again. How are budgets useful when thinking about the past?

Listening

6 🎧 Listen to a conversation between a manager and an accountant. Choose the correct answers.

1. What is the dialogue mostly about?
   A why the budget was exceeded
   B steps for making a budget
   C routine spending patterns
   D techniques for estimating costs

2. Accountants use estimates with
   A some costs.   C spending levels.
   B low forecasts.   D short-term budgets.

7 🎧 Listen again and complete the conversation.

Accountant:	All right, next let's look at our costs. We have to adjust our costs in order to maximize our profits.
Manager:	Hmm ... that's 1 _____ _____ _____ .
Accountant:	Yes, it is. We'll have to use estimates and 2 _____ _____ with some of the costs.
Manager:	OK, then what?
Accountant:	Then we adjust costs according to our sales forecasts.
Manager:	So we might have to look for 3 _____ _____ _____ our costs if the sales forecasts are low?
Accountant:	Exactly. And if the forecasts are high, we might be able to increase our spending 4 _____ _____ _____ .
Manager:	But 5 _____ _____ _____ _____ _____ increase our profits, right?
Accountant:	Of course. 6 _____ _____ _____ _____ of budgeting.

Speaking

8 With a partner, act out the roles below based on Task 7. Then switch roles.

USE LANGUAGE SUCH AS:
Let's look at ...
We might have to ...
Then we adjust ...

Student A: You are making a budget. Talk to Student B about:
• steps for budgeting
• forecasts
• adjusting costs

Student B: You are an accountant. Answer Student A's questions.

Writing

9 You are a manager. Use the passage and the conversation from Task 8 to write notes about the steps for making a budget. Talk about:
• forecasts
• estimating certain costs
• adjusting the budget to maximize profits

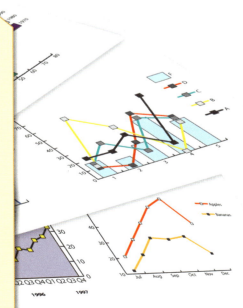

7 Auditing

Get ready!

1 Before you read the passage, talk about these questions.

1. Why do businesses get audited?
2. What are some of the problems that show up in audits?

Reading

2 Read this letter. Then, choose the correct answers.

1. What is the passage mainly about?
   A the results of an audit
   B how to make material adjustments
   C the results of a meeting with the COO.
   D problems with Thomas and Riley's books

2. What did Endless Magic's salespeople do?
   A They made a clerical error.
   B They falsified sales information.
   C They made material adjustments.
   D They showed professional skepticism.

3. What did the company do when it purchased new equipment?
   A It depreciated the equipment.
   B It capitalized its old equipment.
   C It wrote off the purchase as an expense.
   D It got advice from a government employee.

Vocabulary

3 Match the words or phrases (1-5) with the definitions (A-E).

1. __ anomalous
2. __ cutoff point
3. __ chief operating officer
4. __ impropriety
5. __ professional skepticism

A a corporate executive in charge of operations
B the level that must be reached to receive some reward
C the critical attitude an auditor must have
D any activity that is unethical
E out of the ordinary

FROM: Patrick Stevens, Auditor, Thomas and Riley LLP
TO: Jack Riley, Thomas and Riley LLP

Mr. Riley,

I have completed my audit of Endless Magic Toy Company. Unfortunately, I cannot give a **clean opinion** of this company without **material adjustments** to the financial statements. I found a few **anomalous** entries in its books that should be attended to.

First, I noticed that the reported sales figures do not match the actual revenue. At first, I thought it could have been a simple **clerical error**. But then I recalled something I had read earlier about bonuses for sales people. Sure enough, it appears the sales people reported **erroneous** sales figures — sales that won't actually occur until next quarter. I believe they did this in order to surpass the bonus **cutoff point**.

The second **impropriety** that I found had to do with some new manufacturing equipment. As you know, these assets should have been **capitalized** and depreciated over their useful life. But someone chose to write the entire purchase price off as an expense. Any government tax department employee would see this immediately in an audit.

I am surprised by the lack of **professional skepticism** on the part of Endless Magic Toy Company's internal auditor. I have a meeting with the **Chief Operating Officer** tomorrow, and I plan to discuss these issues with her.

Regards,
Patrick Stevens

erroneous

16

4 Fill in the blanks with the correct words or phrases from the word bank.

WORD BANK

clean opinion   erroneous   capitalized
clerical error   material adjustments

1. It wasn't a deliberate falsification, just a(n) _____.
2. Depreciable assets should be _____.
3. The auditor gave the company a(n) _____ because of its accurate records.
4. Ben was fired for recording _____ sales figures.
5. They made _____ to correct the incorrect entries.

5 Listen and read the letter again. What was the auditor surprised by?

Listening

6 Listen to a conversation between an auditor and a COO. Mark the following statements as true (T) or false (F).

1. ___ The woman capitalized her company's new machines.
2. ___ The salespeople lied about reaching the cutoff point.
3. ___ The woman doesn't want to follow GAAP.

7 Listen again and complete the conversation.

Auditor: Well, there are a few things we need to discuss.
COO: OK. 1 _____.
Auditor: First of all, there seems to be a problem with the sales people 2 _____.
COO: Wow. Are you sure about that?
Auditor: Yes, completely sure. 3 _____ actual revenue to the sales reports.
COO: Why would they do that?
Auditor: Well, it looks to me like they were 4 _____ _____ that they 5 _____.
COO: I'm definitely going to 6 _____. What else do we need to discuss?

Speaking

8 With a partner, act out the roles below based on Task 7. Then switch roles.

USE LANGUAGE SUCH AS:

First of all, there seems to be ...
Are you sure about that?
I'm definitely going to ...

Student A: You are a COO of a company that just got audited. Talk to Student B about:
- results of the audit
- false sales reports

Student B: You are an auditor. Answer Student A's questions.

Writing

9 You are an accountant. Use the letter and the conversation from Task 8 to write a brief letter to one of the company's executives about an audit that you performed. Talk about:
- whether or not you can give a clean opinion
- anomalous entries

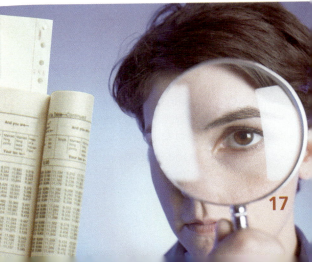

8 The Break-even Point

Get ready!

1 Before you read the passage, talk about these questions.

1. What is the break-even point?
2. Why is the break-even point important?

optimal price

delicate balance

From: Lauren Archer, CPA
To: Floyd Hatcher

Mr. Hatcher,

You asked about how to maximize profits. The best advice I can offer is to know your break-even point. This is the amount of revenue you need to cover your costs and break even. It's easy to calculate your **break even point**. You just have to know your variable costs and your fixed costs.

First, figure out your **margin ratio**. This is simply margin divided by revenue. For example, if you generated $1,000 in revenue and your margin was $300, then your margin ratio would be:

$$300 \div 1000 = 0.3$$

Now you're ready to calculate your break-even point. Divide your fixed costs by your margin ratio. Let's say that your fixed costs were **locked in** at $500. Your break even point would be:

$$500 \div 0.3 = 1667$$

So, if your fixed expenses were $500, you would need to generate $1,667 to **recoup** those expenses and break even.

You can use this formula to help you set **optimal** prices and sales goals for marketing. But you must be careful. If your revenue **slumps** below the break-even point, you will be in the **loss zone**. It takes a **delicate** balance between pricing and costs to push your revenues above the break-even point and into the **profit zone**.

lock in

profit zone

loss zone

Reading

2 Read this email. Then mark the following statements as true (T) or false (F).

1 ___ The margin ratio is revenue over margin.
2 ___ The break-even point decreases as the margin ratio decreases.
3 ___ In the situation described above, $1,677 in revenue would result in $10 of profit.

Vocabulary

3 Match the words or phrases (1-5) with the definitions (A-E).

1 ___ recoup   3 ___ profit zone   5 ___ slump
2 ___ optimal 4 ___ loss zone

A to go down
B to regain what was lost
C all amounts of revenue below the break-even point
D all amounts of revenue above the break-even point
E the best possible

4 Fill in the blanks with the correct words or phrases: *margin ratio*, *break-even point*, *locked in*, *delicate*.

1. Divide fixed costs by the _____ to see how much revenue you need.
2. The company suffered losses since its revenue was below its _____ .
3. Clearly, variable expenses cannot be _____ like fixed expenses can.
4. It's difficult to find that _____ stability between prices and costs.

5 🎧 Listen and read the email again. What must companies balance to make a profit?

Listening

6 🎧 Listen to a conversation between an accountant and her client. Choose the correct answers.

1. What is the dialogue mostly about?
   A challenging competitors
   B lowering the margin ratio
   C guarding against rising costs
   D lowering the break-even point

2. Decreasing variable expenses would result in
   A less revenue.
   B less competition.
   C a higher margin ratio.
   D a higher break-even point.

7 🎧 Listen again and complete the conversation.

A: Higher prices would mean higher revenue and a larger margin ratio.
C: Oh, right, I see. A higher margin ratio would lower the break-even point.
A: Right. Although raising prices sometimes lowers revenue because people 1 _____ _____ _____ _____ .
C: Yeah, I can't do that. I have a lot of competition. 2 _____ _____ _____ if I raised prices too much.
A: OK. Another option is to lower your fixed costs, if you can.
C: Hmm ... I don't think I can. I mean, 3 _____ _____ _____ _____ my rent or electric bills lowered?
A: Yeah, that's not an option 4 _____ _____ _____ .
C: So, are there any other options?
A: Well, 5 _____ _____ _____ to lower your variable expenses?
C: You mean 6 _____ _____ _____ _____ cheaper production methods?

Speaking

8 With a partner, act out the roles below based on Task 7. Then switch roles.

USE LANGUAGE SUCH AS:
One option is to ...
Another option is to ...
Are there any other options?

Student A: You want to lower your break-even point. Talk to Student B about:
- options for lowering your break-even point
- reasons you can/cannot choose each option

Student B: You are an accountant. Answer Student A's questions.

Writing

9 You are an accountant. Use the email and the conversation from Task 8 to write a brief email to your client explaining a few ways to lower the break-even point. Talk about:
- raising prices
- lowering fixed costs
- lowering variable costs

9 Globalization

Should Accounting Rules be Globalized?
by Harold Mays

The world is shrinking. Due to the **worldwide trend** of globalization, companies all over the world are interacting and doing business with one another. This has led many to suggest that there is a need for **globalized standards** in accounting. A few organizations, like the International Accounting Standards Committee (IASC) and the **International Accounting Standards Commitee (IASC)**, have already begun to design such rules. Many businesses have voluntarily **adopted** these guidelines. Should these or other rules be **applied globally**?

Globalized accounting rules would carry certain advantages. Since this transition is probably **inevitable**, businesses must engage the global market if they wish to maximize their prospects. Indeed, globalization allows for the **free circulation** of capital as well as ideas and innovations. Furthermore, with standardized accounting, companies would be better able to make **strategic decisions** within the global economy.

However, globalization may carry certain disadvantages as well. It may be relatively easy and profitable for large corporations to adjust to globalized standards. But the adjustment would be more difficult for **mid-sized** and small businesses. They have fewer resources than the larger companies. Changing to a new standardized accounting system could be very costly for them. It would require new staff as well as training for existing staff.

...

Get ready!

1 Before you read the passage, talk about these questions.

1. What is globalization?
2. How does globalization affect accounting in your country?

Reading

2 Read this article from an accounting journal. Then, mark the following statements as true (T) or false (F) according to the passage.

1 __ Adjusting to global standards would be difficult for large businesses
2 __ Globalization may lead to the free exchange of ideas between countries.
3 __ Many businesses are already required to use the new global rules.

Vocabulary

3 Match the words or phrases (1-5) with the definitions (A-E).

1 __ inevitable
2 __ applied globally
3 __ worldwide trend
4 __ mid-sized
5 __ strategic decisions

A choices made to improve one's situation
B between large and small
C certain to happen
D used all over the world
E a pattern of behavior that happens everywhere

4 Fill in the blanks with the correct words or phrases: *free circulation*, *International Accounting Standards Committee (IASC)*, *adopt*, *globalized standards*.

1 The _____ has designed global accounting rules.
2 Many people want _____ instead of regional rules.
3 Globalization encourages _____ of ideas.
4 Businesses choose whether or not to _____ new rules.

5 🎧 Listen and read the article again. What would be the main benefit of global accounting rules?

Listening

6 🎧 Listen to a conversation between two accountants. Choose the correct answers.

1 What is the dialogue mostly about?
   A training methods around the world
   B global business regulations and licenses
   C the cost of regulating a global economy
   D advantages and disadvantages of global standards

2 The woman thinks globalized standards will
   A be implemented very quickly.
   B encourage international business.
   C cause growth in larger businesses.
   D block the financing of small businesses.

7 🎧 Listen again and complete the conversation.

A1: What? Are you kidding? It would be so much easier to work with companies from all over the world!
A1: Yes, you're right that it would help large companies expand. But it would hurt smaller businesses.
A1: I'm not sure what you mean.
A1: Well, a new standardized accounting system would 1 _____ _____ and probably new employees.
A2: Yeah, it might cost a little to 2 _____ _____ _____. So what?
A1: So small companies don't have as much money. 3 _____ _____ _____ _____.
A2: OK. 4 _____ _____ _____ _____, but I still think it would be good for business. It might take time for everyone to catch up.
A1: Yeah, and some might never catch up.
A2: You know, it 5 _____ _____ _____ what we think anyway.
A1: What do you mean?
A2: 6 _____ _____ _____ _____. I think it's inevitable.

Speaking

8 With a partner, act out the roles below based on Task 7. Then switch roles.

USE LANGUAGE SUCH AS:
It would be ...
It might cost a little ...
I see your point ...

Student A: You are an accountant. Talk to Student B about:
• the idea of global accounting standards
• advantages and disadvantages of global standards

Student B: You are an accountant. Answer Student A's questions.

Writing

9 You are an accountant. Use the article and the conversation from Task 8 to write a brief letter to the editor of an accounting journal. Talk about:

• a recent article saying globalized accounting standards are a good idea
• your opinion agreeing or disagreeing with the article

21

10 Communicating with Clients

Communication in the 21st Century

convenience

body language

verbal cues

tonal cues

There used to be only two ways that accountants could communicate with their clients: telephone calls and face-to-face meetings. Lucky for us, today's technology offers a few more options. But you must consider your clients' needs and preferences when deciding how to **stay in touch** with them.
Each mode of communication has certain advantages.

Email
- **Reflection** – Email allows you and your client to read, reread, and reflect on each other's messages.
- **Record** – Emails provide an automatic record of your correspondence.

Text Message
- **Convenience** – Most people have cell phones with text messaging capabilities.
- **Record** – Like emails, text messages provide an instant record.

Telephone
- **Verbal Cues** – Verbal communication uses **linguistic cues** that are generally absent from written communication, such as **vernacular** and **slang**.
- **Tonal Cues** – Spoken language is often inflected in ways that are impossible with written language. For example, questions are indicated with a rising tone at the end of a sentence.
- **Instant Clarification** – With text messages or email, you and your client may have to wait for replies. With a telephone, questions, answers, and comments are exchanged instantly.

In-person
- **Non-verbal cues** – Facial expressions, hand gestures, and other forms of **body language** all convey messages.
- Instant Clarification

Get ready!

1 Before you read the passage, talk about these questions.

1. What are some of the new forms of communication in the 21st century?
2. How can accountants use modern technology to communicate with their clients?

Reading

2 Read this accounting blog. Then, mark the following statements as true (T) or false (F).

1. __ Text messaging allows for various tonal cues.
2. __ Email gives people time to think about messages.
3. __ The only way to use non-verbal cues is to meet in-person.

Vocabulary

3 Match the words or phrases (1-5) with the definitions (A-E).

1. __ stay in touch   4. __ tonal cues
2. __ reflection   5. __ vernacular
3. __ convenience

A the act of thinking about something
B to regularly communicate
C common, everyday language
D the quality of being easy to use or requiring little effort
E signals sent by raising and lowering vocal pitch

4 Read the sentence pairs. Choose which word or phrase best fits each blank.

1. body language / linguistic cues
   A Only by speaking can people make use of _____.
   B _____ only works if people can see each other.

2. slang / instant clarification
   A Bean counter is a(n) _____ term for "accountant."
   B Lynn only talks by telephone so that there is _____.

3. verbal cues / non-verbal cues
   A _____ include things like facial expressions.
   B _____ are signals that are sent through language.

5 🎧 Listen and read the blog again. What do emails and texts offer that other forms of communication do not?

Listening

6 🎧 Listen to a conversation between two accountants. Choose the correct answers.

1. What is the dialogue mostly about?
   A communicating with a troublesome client
   B lowering telephone and internet expenses
   C teaching a client new communication tools
   D modernizing the office's communication systems

2. What is true about the man's client?
   A He has a busy schedule.
   B He does not have a cell phone.
   C He comes to the office uninvited.
   D He has poor communication skills.

7 🎧 Listen again and complete the conversation.

Accountant 1:	Wow! **1** _____!
Accountant 2:	What's wrong?
Accountant 1:	I'm getting **2** _____ _____ _____ with this new client.
Accountant 2:	What did he do?
Accountant 1:	He only **3** _____ _____ _____ in-person.
Accountant 2:	OK. I do that with a lot of my clients. What's the problem?
Accountant 1:	The problem is that **4** _____ _____ _____, and I don't have time to meet with him **5** _____ _____ _____ _____.
Accountant 2:	Why don't you try **6** _____ _____?

Speaking

8 With a partner, act out the roles below based on Task 7. Then switch roles.

USE LANGUAGE SUCH AS:
What's the problem?
He only likes to communicate ...
Why don't you try ...?

Student A: You are an accountant. Talk to Student B about:
- a client's communication preference
- using other forms of communication

Student B: You are an accountant. Answer Student A's questions.

Writing

9 You are an accountant. Use the blog and the conversation from Task 8 to write a brief email to a client describing several ways that the client may stay in touch with you. Talk about:
- your busy schedule
- email
- telephone
- text messaging

11 Viability

Balance Sheet
As of September 30th, 2015

Assets		Liabilities	
Cash	3,000	Accounts Payable	20,000
Accounts Receivable	2,000	Debts	60,000
Inventory	50,000	Total Liabilities	80,000
Fixed Assets	45,000	Owner's Equity	
		Total Equity	20,000
Total Assets	100,000	Total Liabilities and Equity	100,000

From: Valerie Harris, Head of Acquisitions Department, Kyle and Long Enterprises
To: Derek Chapman, CPA, Kyle and Long Enterprises

Derek,
I'd like to get your opinion on the **viability** of a potential **buyout** I've been working on. It's a medium-sized manufacturing **plant** located on the island of San Gabriel. We've already **raised the capital**. One of our regional managers has a great deal of **local knowledge**, as he is the son of San Gabriel immigrants. He'll be participating in this acquisition in an **advisory** capacity. I've attached some of the current owner's financial statements for you to review. Thank you for your help.
Best wishes, Valerie

From: Derek Chapman, CPA, Kyle and Long Enterprises
To: Valerie Harris, Head of Acquisitions Department, Kyle and Long Enterprises

Hi, Valerie. Unfortunately, I can't approve of this **venture**. I'm concerned that the political instability in San Gabriel would cause problems with **supply and distribution channels**. We simply can't take that risk.
The second issue I'd like to point out to you is that the current owner's inventory level is **astronomical** compared to cash and accounts receivable. It looks like the owner has produced a great deal of inventory and is having trouble selling it.
Thirdly, and finally, are you aware of the fact that one of our major competitors just built a similar plant just forty kilometers to the east? In light of the risks I mentioned above, combined with this powerful regional competitor, I simply don't think it would be **cost effective** to proceed with this acquisition.
Respectfully, Derek Chapman

Get ready!

1 Before you read the passage, talk about these questions.

1 Why might one company buy out another?
2 How can a company decide whether a buyout will be profitable?

Reading

2 Read these emails. Then, mark the following statements as true (T) or false (F).

1 __ Valerie is looking for the funding for the buyout.
2 __ Derek disapproves of Valerie's plan.
3 __ Strong competitive forces already exist in San Gabriel.

Vocabulary

3 Match the words or phrase (1-5) with the definitions (A-E).

1 __ viability   4 __ raise capital
2 __ buyout   5 __ local knowledge
3 __ plant

A the act of purchasing a company
B a building used to manufacture something
C to gather money
D familiarity with a particular region
E the ability to succeed

4 Fill in the blanks with the correct words or phrases from the word bank.

Word BANK

advisory   astronomical
supply and distribution channels
venture   cost effective

1. The company is raising capital for a new _____.
2. Carter is a consultant. He is often hired for _____ positions.
3. The CPAs are analyzing whether the investment will be _____.
4. By expanding _____, a company can deliver products to more customers.
5. The company's struggles to pay its bills because its debt is _____.

5 🎧 Listen and read the emails again. What has recently happened close to the factory Valerie proposes to buy?

Listening

6 🎧 Listen to a conversation between a CPA and an executive. Choose the correct answers.

1. What is the dialogue mostly about?
   A the viability of a venture
   B the company's responsibilities
   C the viability of a local government
   D the analysis of management techniques

2. What is the woman likely to do?
   A go ahead with the buyout
   B talk to government officials
   C think more about the venture
   D ask for another CPA's opinion

7 🎧 Listen again and complete the conversation.

HAD: Well, no. Honestly, I think you were **1** _____ _____ in your analysis.
CPA: Really? Um, what did you disagree with?
HAD: Well, I **2** _____ _____ _____ you think political instability would affect our business.
CPA: Hmm ... well, sometimes corporations think if they **3** _____ _____ _____ _____ _____, politics won't affect them.
HAD: That's **4** _____ _____ _____. I mean, we aren't going to make any political statements.
CPA: But the thing is, if **5** _____ _____ _____, it could end up blocking supply and distribution channels.
HAD: OK, I see your point, but I'm not sure I agree.
CPA: OK. **6** _____ _____ _____: even if I'm wrong about the politics, there's still a problem with debt to equity.

Speaking

8 With a partner, act out the roles below based on Task 7. Then switch roles.

USE LANGUAGE SUCH AS:
I think you were too conservative ...
What did you disagree with?
I'm not sure I agree.

Student A: You are the head of an acquisitions department. Talk to Student B about:
• a potential buyout
• political instability
• the viability of the business

Student B: You are a CPA. Answer Student A's questions.

Writing

9 You are CPA. Use the emails and the conversation from Task 8 to write a brief letter to the head of acquisitions explaining why you do not recommend going ahead with a buyout. Talk about:
• political conditions
• supply and distribution channels
• financial figures–debt, inventory, etc.

12 Buy or Lease?

BUY OR LEASE
by Alex Chavez

Periodically, every business needs new equipment or facilities. Very few have sufficient resources at their disposal to buy these items outright. There are typically only two options: **finance** the purchase or **lease** instead. How can you decide which option will be more profitable?

First, you should understand what a lease is and how it works. Basically, a lease is an agreement in which an owner, or **lessor**, allows someone else, a **lessee**, to use their equipment or property. In exchange, the lessee agrees to pay the lessor some agreed upon amount of money, usually more than the actual value of the property.

There are certain advantages to leasing. The most obvious is the fact that there is no **down-payment**. If you decide instead to purchase property, you will have to finance it. **Financiers** often require down-payments of 25% or more. Additionally, leases offer some protection against equipment obsolescence. If something becomes obsolete, you can simply stop leasing it. However, keep in mind that most leases have penalties for **early termination**.

Leasing also carries certain disadvantages. Although you have use of the property through most of its **useful life**, you lose its **economic value** at the end of the **lease term**. Furthermore, you can sometimes get greater tax benefits through depreciation if you buy instead of lease. You have to **run the numbers** to find out for sure.

Business Edition – Spring Issue, P. 19

Get ready!

1 Before you read the passage, talk about these questions.

1. What things do companies buy and lease?
2. How can a company decide whether to buy or lease a particular item?

Reading

2 Read this article in a business magazine. Then mark the following statements as true (T) or false (F).

1. __ Lessors often require a 25% down-payment.
2. __ The total cost of a lease is usually greater than the asset's value.
3. __ Buying is a good way to get tax benefits through depreciation.

Vocabulary

3 Match the words or phrases (1-5) with the definitions (A-E).

1. __ finance
2. __ lease
3. __ useful life
4. __ early termination
5. __ down-payment

A. an agreement in which one person pays to borrow another's property
B. the act of ending a lease prematurely
C. to borrow money in order to purchase something
D. the length of time in which an item can be used
E. a percentage of an item's total value that must be paid before receiving a loan

4 Read the sentence pairs. Choose which word or phrase best fits each blank.

1 financier / lease term
   A Payments will be made in monthly increments throughout the _____ .
   B The _____ requires a 20% down-payment.

2 lessee / economic value
   A The _____ agrees to return the property in good condition.
   B Most products retain _____ even at the end of their useful lives.

3 run the numbers / lessor
   A _____ to see which deal would be better.
   B The _____ retains ownership throughout the lease term.

5 🎧 Listen and read the article again. What are the disadvantages of leasing something?

Listening

6 🎧 Listen to a conversation between an accountant and his client. Choose the correct answers.

1 What is the dialogue mostly about?
   A reasons to lease or not
   B how many vehicles to buy
   C problems with the current lease
   D why the woman needs vehicles

2 How can the woman maximize her liquidity?
   A by selling fleet vehicles
   B by leasing fleet vehicles
   C by postponing her purchase
   D by getting vehicles that last a long time

7 🎧 Listen again and complete the conversation.

Client: I really need to figure out 1 _____ _____ _____ my cash on hand.
Accountant: OK. So you need to have 2 _____ _____ ?
Client: Right. But, the thing is, I also need to make 3 _____ _____ _____ – fleet vehicles.
Accountant: Wow. Yeah, that 4 _____ _____ _____ a lot of your cash. What about leasing?
Client: Leasing? No, I don't want to 5 _____ _____ _____ on lease payments.
Accountant: Um, well, I'm not sure you really 6 _____ _____ _____ of leasing.

Speaking

8 With a partner, act out the roles below based on Task 7. Then switch roles.

USE LANGUAGE SUCH AS:
I really need to figure out how to ...
So you need to have more ...?
That's a good point.

Student A: You need to make a purchase but also maximize liquidity. Talk to Student B about:
• whether you should buy or lease

Student B: You are an accountant. Answer Student A's questions.

Writing

9 You are an accountant. Use the article and the conversation from Task 8 to write a brief email to you client recommending that he or she buy/lease new vehicles. Explain why. Talk about:

• advantages and disadvantages of buying
• advantages and disadvantages of leasing

13 Tax Havens

Get ready!

1 Before you read the passage, talk about these questions.

1. Do businesses and people pay higher taxes as they make higher profits in your country?
2. How can companies avoid paying taxes?

Haven on Earth: The Best Place in the World to Move Your Business!

Hundreds of people are convicted of **tax evasion** every year. Don't let it happen to you! Move your business to a place where it won't be punished for making a profit!

Haven Island is the perfect location from which to operate your business without fear of unfair **tax avoidance** laws. Our government refuses to **levy** any excessive taxes. We won't **impose** extra fees on your business simply for being successful. Furthermore, we offer huge **tax breaks** to existing firms that wish to relocate here. But that's not all…

Do you live in a country with multiple **tax brackets**? Many people call such tax policies "**progressive taxation**," but we call it WRONG! That's why Haven Island has adopted a **flat tax** for all businesses and individuals. But wait; there's more…

Do you prefer to stay in another country, but still want to invest in the prosperity that is Haven Island? Many countries impose fees or taxes on funds invested in a foreign country. That's why our biggest **business association**, The Free Capital Association, has decided to help **promote** investment by foreign firms. It has offered to pay at least 50% of your fees and taxes when you invest in a Haven Island company.

Reading

2 Read this advertisement. Then, mark the following statements as true (T) or false (F).

1. ___ The Free Capital Association approves of progressive taxation.
2. ___ Businesses that move to Haven Island will have to pay a flat tax.
3. ___ Haven Island's government created the Free Capital Association.

Vocabulary

3 Match the words or phrases (1-5) with the definitions (A-E).

1. ___ promote
2. ___ tax evasion
3. ___ levy
4. ___ business association
5. ___ tax breaks

A. to encourage or stimulate
B. to impose something
C. the act of avoiding paying money that is owed to a government
D. a voluntary union of companies
E. discounts that are designed to encourage certain behaviors

4 Fill in the blanks with the correct words or phrases from the word bank.

Word BANK

tax avoidance   flat tax
progressive taxation
tax bracket   impose

1 In an obvious case of _____, the CEO moved the company overseas.
2 Some countries _____ few taxes as a way to promote business.
3 With _____, citizens pay incrementally more as their income increases.
4 A _____ charges all tax payers at the same rate.
5 Harris paid more in taxes than Judy since he was in a higher _____.

5 🎧 Listen and read the advertisement again. What incentive exists to invest in a company on Haven Island?

Listening

6 🎧 Listen to a conversation between two accountants. Choose the correct answers.

1 What is the dialogue mostly about?
   A implementing new tax laws
   B increasing regional revenue
   C an opportunity to pay less in taxes
   D a law that gives tax breaks in the UK

2 What ethical concern does the man mention?
   A paying no tax on revenue
   B paying extremely low wages
   C abandoning the local workforce
   D giving tax breaks to only certain businesses

7 🎧 Listen again and complete the conversation.

Accountant 1:	Yeah, it looks like the government of Haven Island is **1** _____ _____ _____ that.
Accountant 2:	Good for them. **2** _____ _____ _____ do they have?
Accountant 1:	Well, **3** _____ _____ _____ they also offer tax breaks to businesses that move there.
Accountant 2:	Wow. **4** _____ _____ _____ _____ _____ move there.
Accountant 1:	I **5** _____ _____ the same thing.
Accountant 2:	But, you know, I'm not sure that would be ethical.
Accountant 1:	Why would it not be ethical?
Accountant 2:	Well, there's **6** _____ _____ _____ that all our customers would still be here in the UK.

Speaking

8 With a partner, act out the roles below based on Task 7. Then switch roles.

USE LANGUAGE SUCH AS:
What other policies do they have?
I'm not sure ...
Why would it not ...?

Student A: You are an accountant. Talk to Student B about:
- a country with favorable tax policies
- whether or not to move your business to that country
- whether or not it would be ethical to take advantage of the country's tax policies

Student B: You are an accountant. Answer Student A's questions.

Writing

9 You are an accountant. Use the advertisement and the conversation from Task 8 to write an email to a coworker explaining why you think you should/should not move your business to Haven Island. Talk about:
- flat taxes
- tax breaks
- ethics

14 Tax Accounting

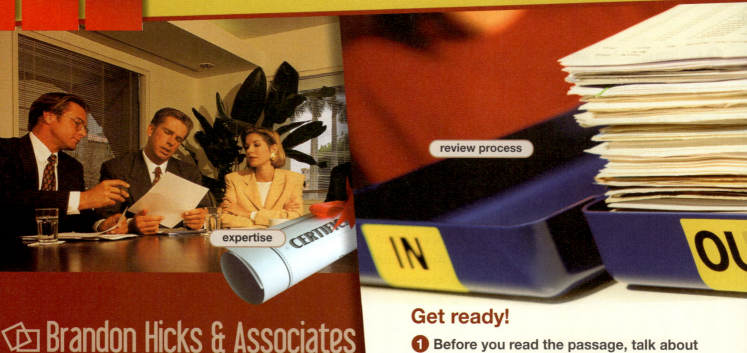

Brandon Hicks & Associates
PROFESSIONAL TAX ACCOUNTING

Filling out tax forms is **tedious** and often confusing. Why not let our experience and **expertise** work for you?

At Brandon Hicks and Associates, we know how important it is to prepare your taxes quickly, efficiently, and correctly. All of our CPAs have a minimum of five years' experience in individual and business tax accounting. But don't take our word for it. We highly recommend that you check with the **board of accountancy** to verify the status of our CPAs.

Not only will you benefit from our years of knowledge and experience, but you can also rest assured that you won't pay more than you have to. No matter how complex your situation, we guarantee to maximize your savings. All of our work is done **in-house** – nothing is **outsourced**. In addition, we have a proven **review process**. Every completed tax form is **evaluated** by a senior accountant before filing.

As important as accuracy is, we understand that privacy and security are equally important. And of course, we'll never share your personal information with **third parties**. Our **privacy policy** is among the strictest in the business. Your information will not be shared with anyone except our **quality assurance** personnel.

Get ready!

1 Before you read the passage, talk about these questions.

1. How do tax accounting firms find clients?
2. What are some selling points to mention when advertising an accounting firm?

Reading

2 Read this promotional literature for a tax accounting firm. Then, mark the following statements as true (T) or false (F).

1. __ Brandon Hicks and Associates doesn't contract out any of its work.
2. __ The board of accountancy created a tax review process used by the firm.
3. __ Tax accountants need at least five years' experience to work at the firm.

Vocabulary

3 Match the words or phrases (1-5) with the definitions (A-E).

1. __ third party
2. __ expertise
3. __ evaluate
4. __ board of accountancy
5. __ quality assurance

A a great amount of knowledge and experience
B a governing body that verifies CPA credentials
C a division of employees that monitor a company's performance
D someone other than the two principal parties in an agreement
E to test or perform an assessment of something

4 Fill in the blanks with the correct words or phrases from the word bank.

WORD BANK

review process   in-house
tedious   outsource
privacy policy

1 Doing repetitious paperwork can be very _____ .
2 Accounting firms should have a _____ to ensure accuracy.
3 A _____ informs clients how their personal information will be handled.
4 Many companies _____ certain jobs to save money.
5 Some firms don't outsource; they perform all work _____ .

5 Listen and read the promotional literature again. Who checks completed tax forms for accuracy?

Listening

6 Listen to a conversation between an accountant and a potential client. Choose the correct answers.

1 What is the dialogue mostly about?
   A why the firm outsources
   B changing an appointment
   C correcting the woman's records
   D a company's operational procedures

2 What did the woman's previous accountant do?
   A went out of business
   B made an error on her taxes
   C failed to renew his credentials
   D shared her personal information

7 Listen again and complete the conversation.

Accountant:	That's correct. And you would be able to 1 _____ to the CPA working on your files.
Caller:	OK. 2 _____ ? I think my old accountant got my name on some mailing list.
Accountant:	Well, you definitely don't have to worry about that with us. We 3 _____ with third parties.
Caller:	Is there a way I could 4 _____ of your CPAs?
Accountant:	Yes, ma'am. In fact we encourage it. All you have to do is check with the accountancy board.
Caller:	OK. It's just that I'm in a really 5 _____ right now.
Accountant:	I understand. I guarantee we can handle it.
Caller:	Well, I think I'd like to 6 _____ .

Speaking

8 With a partner, act out the roles below based on Task 7. Then switch roles.

USE LANGUAGE SUCH AS:

What about privacy?
You don't have to worry about that with us.
I guarantee we can ...

Student A: You are calling an accounting firm. Talk to Student B about:
• the firm's privacy policy
• how to verify the status of the firm's CPA's

Student B: You are an accountant. Answer Student A's questions.

Writing

9 You are a potential client. Use the promotional literature and the conversation from Task 8 to write notes about the accounting firm. Talk about:
• services the firm provides
• the firm's privacy policy
• the CPAs' credentials and experience
• whether or not the firm outsources

15 The Future of Accounting

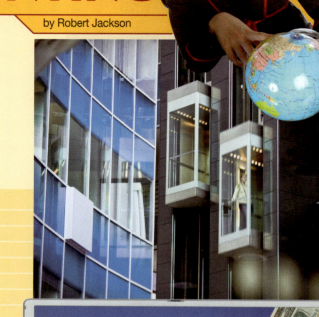

American Accounting Journal – Issue 19, 20th Edition - Page 42

THE FUTURE OF ACCOUNTING

by Robert Jackson

Traditionally, accounting has been a relatively narrow profession. There were only a few potential career paths. Accountants generally worked in **public practice** for accounting firms, or as financial record-keepers in private businesses. But societal and economic changes are bringing new opportunities.

Many countries in the world have transitioned from manufacturing and production to a **service-based economy**. This shift is opening the doors to a variety of new opportunities. In addition to the traditional **attest services** accountants perform (such as **audit opinions**), accountants will be in greater demand in the following areas:

- Strategic Planning
- **Mergers**
- **Acquisitions**
- **Litigation Support**
- Financial Services/Investments
- Audit Fraud
- **Risk Assessment**
- **Electronic Commerce**

In addition to the broadening applications of accounting skills, the day-to-day working conditions are evolving as well. Technological advancements, particularly communications, allow accountants a great deal of **flextime** and **flex location**.

In conclusion, the prospects are bright. The opportunities are expanding. The working conditions are becoming more favorable. There is even a growing perception of accountants as business partners, rather than back-office bean counters. Indeed, numbers are the language of business; and no one is more fluent in that language than accountants.

electronic commerce

Get ready!

1 Before you read the passage, talk about these questions.

1. What are some of the traditional jobs that accountants have worked?
2. What jobs will accountants do in the future?

Reading

2 Read this article in an accounting journal. Then, mark the following statements as true (T) or false (F).

1. __ There is a growing demand for accountants to check the work of auditors.
2. __ Accountants are required to work very strict schedules.
3. __ Accountants help attorneys and other professionals in the legal field.

Vocabulary

3 Match the words or phrases (1-6) with the definitions (A-F).

1. __ merger
2. __ acquisition
3. __ flextime
4. __ flex location
5. __ attest services
6. __ litigation support

A tasks in which accountants offer their professional opinion
B a joining of companies
C a takeover of one company by another
D the ability to work anywhere
E accounting services within the legal profession
F the ability to work any schedule

4 Fill in the blanks with the correct words or phrases from the word bank.

WORD BANK
public practice   service-based economy
audit opinion   risk assessment
electronic commerce

1. Before moving ahead with the merger, have a CPA perform a(n) _____.
2. The accountant reviewed all the books and is ready to give her _____.
3. In a(n) _____, knowledge is the most important asset an individual can have.
4. Most accountants still work in _____ jobs like tax preparation.
5. The Internet has created a whole new market of _____.

5 🎧 Listen and read the article again. What has brought new opportunities for accountants?

Listening

6 🎧 Listen to a conversation between two accountants. Choose the correct answers.

1. What is the dialogue mostly about?
   A moving the office overseas
   B new job opportunities in accounting
   C problems resulting from globalization
   D plans to merge with a partner company

2. How will involvement in risk assessment change the role of accountants?
   A They will get promoted faster.
   B They will likely earn higher bonuses.
   C They will be involved in decision making.
   D They will have more educational requirements.

7 🎧 Listen again and complete the conversation.

A2: Well, I feel that all the standardized rules will make our job tedious and boring.
A1: No, I disagree. Globalization is 1 _____ of new opportunities for accountants.
A2: 2 _____. We'll still be stuck in back offices 3 _____.
A1: No, really, there are so many new career 4 _____ to us.
A2: What kind of options?
A1: Well, for example, a lot of companies are using accountants for things like risk assessment.
A2: Risk assessment? So does that mean 5 _____ in decision making?
A1: Uh-huh. I'm telling you, globalization is opening 6 _____.
A2: Wow. That's great.

Speaking

8 With a partner, act out the roles below based on Task 7. Then switch roles.

USE LANGUAGE SUCH AS:
Globalization is opening up ...
I doubt it. We'll still be stuck in ...
No, really, there are so many ...

Student A: You are an accountant. Talk to Student B about:
- the effect of globalization on accounting
- new career opportunities for accountants

Student B: You are an accountant. Answer Student A's questions.

Writing

9 You are an accountant. Use the article and the conversation from Task 8 to write a journal entry about your future goals as an accountant. Talk about:
- career opportunities
- your job preferences
- your career goals

33

Glossary

acquisition [N-COUNT-U15] An **acquisition** is the act of one company absorbing another.

activity-based costing [N-PHRASE-U5] **Activity-based costing** is a method for allocating indirect costs as parts of production costs.

administrative leave [N-UNCOUNT-U3] **Administrative leave** is a condition in which an employee is not allowed to come to work.

adopt [V-T-U9] To **adopt** something is to decide to use it.

advisory [ADJ-U11] If something is **advisory**, its purpose is to provide guidance.

anomalous [ADJ-U7] If something is **anomalous**, it is out of the ordinary.

apply (something) **globally** [V-PHRASE-U9] To **apply** something **globally** is to make it a regular policy all over the world.

astronomical [ADJ-U11] If something is **astronomical**, it is very large.

attest service [N-COUNT-U15] An **attest service** is a service performed by an accountant in which the accountant offers his or her professional opinion about something (e.g., an audit opinion).

audit opinion [N-COUNT-U15] An **audit opinion** is the professional opinion of an accountant regarding the results of an audit.

bar [V-T-U4] To **bar** something is to exclude or not consider it.

board of accountancy [N-UNCOUNT-U14] The **board of accountancy** is a governing body that oversees CPAs.

body language [N-UNCOUNT-U10] **Body language** is the way that people send signals with their bodies (e.g., facial expressions).

break-even point [N-UNCOUNT-U8] **Break-even point** is the level at which revenue equals costs.

bribery [N-UNCOUNT-U3] **Bribery** is the act of giving someone money in exchange for favorable treatment.

business association [N-COUNT-U13] A **business association** is a voluntary union of businesses.

business budgeting [N-UNCOUNT-U6] **Business budgeting** is the act of creating a budget for a business.

buyout [N-COUNT-U11] A **buyout** is the act of purchasing a company.

capitalize [V-T-U7] To **capitalize** something is to record it as an asset.

catastrophe [N-COUNT-U4] A **catastrophe** is a disaster or event that causes a lot of damage.

chief operating officer (COO) [N-COUNT-U7] A **chief operating officer** is a corporate executive who is in charge of a company's operations.

clean opinion [N-PHRASE-U7] A **clean opinion** is a statement by an auditor saying that a company's records have no improprieties.

clerical error [N-COUNT-U7] A **clerical error** is an unintentional mistake made while doing paperwork.

combine [V-T-U1] To **combine** things is to put them together.

concrete goal [N-COUNT-U6] A **concrete goal** is a well-defined achievement to pursue.

convenience [N-UNCOUNT-U10] **Convenience** is the state of being easy, useful, and comfortable.

convention [N-COUNT-U1] A **convention** is a generally accepted policy or pattern of behavior.

cooking the books [N-PHRASE-U3] **Cooking the books** is the act of recording false information to hide some illegal activity.

cost driver [N-COUNT-U5] **Cost drivers** are categories of production costs into which indirect costs are allocated.

cost effective [ADJ-U11] If something is **cost effective**, it will generate sufficient income in comparison to how much was invested in it.

creditor [N-COUNT-U2] A **creditor** is someone to whom money is owed.

current ratio [N-UNCOUNT-U4] A **current ratio** is the result of dividing a company's assets by its liabilities.

custom [N-COUNT-U1] A **custom** is a generally accepted pattern of behavior.

cutoff point [N-COUNT-U7] A **cutoff point** is the level that must be reached in order to receive some reward.

debt-to-equity ratio [N-COUNT-U2] The **debt-to-equity ratio** is a comparison of how much a company owes to how much it is worth.

delicate [ADJ-U8] If something is **delicate**, it is easily damaged, changed, or broken.

direct cost [N-COUNT-U5] A **direct cost** is an expense that rises and falls with the volume of production.

direct labor [N-UNCOUNT-U5] **Direct labor** is the wages of employees who make a company's products.

direct materials [N-COUNT-U5] **Direct materials** are the materials that are used to make products.

double underline [N-COUNT-U1] A **double underline** is two lines under a number indicating the bottom line or most important part(s) of a financial statement.

down-payment [N-COUNT-U12] A **down-payment** is a percentage of an item's total value that must be paid at the time of purchase in order to finance the rest of the purchase price.

early termination [N-UNCOUNT-U12] **Early termination** is the act of ending a lease prior to the end of the lease term.

electronic commerce [N-UNCOUNT-U15] **Electronic commerce** is business that is conducted via computers and the Internet.

erroneous [ADJ-U7] If something is **erroneous**, it is false.

evaluate [V-T-U14] To **evaluate** something is to test it.

expertise [N-UNCOUNT-U14] **Expertise** is a high level of knowledge and experience within a given field.

finance [V-T-U12] To **finance** something is to borrow money in order to purchase it.

financier [N-COUNT-U12] A **financier** is someone who lends money.

fixed cost [N-COUNT-U5] A **fixed cost** is an expense that stays the same regardless of the volume of production.

fixed overhead [N-COUNT-U5] **Fixed overheads** are costs such as rents and insurance premiums that stay the same regardless of the volume of production.

Glossary

flat tax [N-UNCOUNT-U13] A **flat tax** is a system in which everyone pays the same rate of tax no matter how much they make.

flex location [N-UNCOUNT-U15] **Flex location** is the ability to work from any location.

flextime [N-UNCOUNT-U15] **Flextime** is the ability to work any schedule.

forecast [N-COUNT-U6] A **forecast** is a prediction about the future.

free circulation [N-UNCOUNT-U9] **Free circulation** is the act of transferring things broadly and without restraint.

fundamental analysis [N-UNCOUNT-U2] **Fundamental analysis** is a series of evaluations performed to determine a company's value and growth potential.

general and administrative costs [N-PHRASE-U1] **General and administrative costs** are the amounts paid for basic business operations.

globalized standard [N-COUNT-U9] A **globalized standard** is a rule that is applied all over the world.

growth potential [N-UNCOUNT-U2] **Growth potential** is the ability of a business to expand.

impose [V-T-U13] To **impose** something is to forcefully require it.

impropriety [N-COUNT-U7] An **impropriety** is any activity that is unethical.

indicator [N-COUNT-U4] An **indicator** is a sign or trait that reveals something about a person or company.

indirect cost [N-COUNT-U5] An **indirect cost** is an expense that stays the same regardless of the volume of production.

inevitable [ADJ-U9] If something is **inevitable**, it is certain to happen.

in-house [ADV-U14] Is something is done **in-house**, it is done only by employees of a particular company.

instant clarification [N-UNCOUNT-U10] **Instant clarification** is the ability to elaborate on messages immediately.

insurance premium [N-COUNT-U1] An **insurance premium** is a fee that is paid for financial protection.

International Accounting Standards Committee (IASC) [N-UNCOUNT-U9] The **IASC** is a governing body that has designed a set of global accounting rules.

involuntary bankruptcy [N-UNCOUNT-U4] **Involuntary bankruptcy** is a bankruptcy petition made by creditors who are seeking to get money back from a company that cannot pay its debts to them.

jargon [N-UNCOUNT-U1] **Jargon** is language that is only used by a certain group of people.

juggling the accounts [N-PHRASE-U3] **Juggling the accounts** is the act of recording false information.

lease [V-T-U12] To **lease** something is to pay to use it for a period of time.

lease term [N-COUNT-U12] A **lease term** is the period of time until a lease expires.

lessee [N-COUNT-U12] A **lessee** is a person who leases property.

lessor [N-COUNT-U12] A **lessor** is a person who owns leased property.

levy [V-T-U13] To **levy** something is to impose it.

linguistic cues [N-COUNT-U10] **Linguistic cues** are signals that are sent through patterns in language.

litigation support [N-UNCOUNT-U15] **Litigation support** is an accounting field in which an accountant assists law professionals.

local knowledge [N-UNCOUNT-U11] **Local knowledge** is familiarity with a particular region.

locked in [ADJ-U8] If something is **locked in**, it cannot change.

long-term [ADJ-U6] If something is **long-term**, it is taking place over a lengthy period of time.

loss zone [N-UNCOUNT-U8] The **loss zone** is a state in which a company spends more money than it earns.

making false entries [N-PHRASE-U3] **Making false entries** is the act of intentionally recording incorrect information.

margin ratio [N-UNCOUNT-U8] **Margin ratio** is margin divided by revenue.

material adjustment [N-COUNT-U7] A **material adjustment** is an entry that is recorded to correct an incorrect or false entry.

merger [N-COUNT-U15] A **merger** is the joining of two companies.

mid-sized [ADJ-U9] If something is **mid-sized**, it is between large and small.

minus sign [N-COUNT-U1] A **minus sign** is the mathematical symbol that indicates subtraction.

model [N-COUNT-U6] A **model** is a representation of something that is expected to happen.

money-laundering [N-UNCOUNT-U3] **Money-laundering** is the act of directing money through a corporation to hide illegal activity.

near-term [ADJ-U6] If something is **near-term**, it is taking place over a small period of time.

negative outlook [N-PHRASE-U6] A **negative outlook** is a gloomy view of the future.

non-verbal cues [N-COUNT-U10] **Non-verbal cues** are signals that are sent without using sound.

operating cycle [N-COUNT-U4] An **operating cycle** is the pattern of purchasing materials and using them to earn a profit.

optimal [ADJ-U8] If something is **optimal**, it is of the best possible nature for a situation.

outsource [V-T-U14] To **outsource** work is to hire people from outside a company to do the company's work.

plant [N-COUNT-U11] A **plant** is a building used to manufacture something.

positive outlook [N-PHRASE-U6] A **positive outlook** is an optimistic view of the future.

privacy policy [N-COUNT-U14] A **privacy policy** is a formal statement of how a company will handle its clients' private information.

professional skepticism [N-PHRASE-U7] **Professional skepticism** is the critical attitude that auditors must have when reviewing records.

profit zone [N-UNCOUNT-U8] The **profit zone** is a state in which a company earns more than it spends.

progressive taxation [N-UNCOUNT-U13] **Progressive taxation** is a system in which high-income earners are required to pay a higher tax rate than low-income earners.

promote [V-T-U13] To **promote** something is to encourage or stimulate its growth.

Glossary

public practice [N-UNCOUNT-U15] **Public practice** consists of any field of accounting, such as tax preparation, in which the accountant works with the general public.

quality assurance [N-UNCOUNT-U14] **Quality assurance** is a group of employees within an organization that monitor the organization's operations, records, etc.

raise capital [V-PHRASE-U11] To **raise capital** is to gather money.

recoup [V-T-U8] To **recoup** expenses is to pay back money that was spent.

reflection [N-UNCOUNT-U10] **Reflection** is the act of thinking about something.

repetitive [ADJ-U4] If something is **repetitive**, it happens over and over.

reroute [V-T-U3] To **reroute** something is to direct it to a different destination.

review process [N-UNCOUNT-U14] A **review process** is a procedure in which documents are inspected for accuracy.

risk assessment [N-UNCOUNT-U15] **Risk assessment** is an accounting field in which an accountant analyzes business activities and determines the risks associated with them.

run the numbers [V-PHRASE-U12] To **run the numbers** is to make calculations in order to analyze one or more scenarios.

sales-skimming [N-UNCOUNT-U3] **Sales-skimming** is the act of taking money from an employer's revenue.

second-nature [ADJ-U1] If something is **second-nature**, it has been practiced so much that it can be done with little or no thought.

security valuation [N-UNCOUNT-U2] **Security valuation** is the act of setting stock prices.

service-based economy [N-UNCOUNT-U15] A **service-based economy** is a system in which most of the workforce works in jobs that require knowledge and customer service skills, rather than physical labor.

short-term [ADJ-U6] If something is **short-term**, it is taking place over a small period of time.

side-by-side comparison [N-COUNT-U2] A **side-by-side comparison** is an evaluation of two things and how they relate to one another.

slang [N-UNCOUNT-U10] **Slang** is casual speech, often including idioms.

slump [V-I-U8] To **slump** is to decrease for a long period.

solvency [N-UNCOUNT-U4] **Solvency** is the ability to pay debts.

statement of financial condition [N-COUNT-U2] A **statement of financial condition** is a balance sheet.

stay in touch [V-PHRASE-U10] To **stay in touch** with someone is to communicate with him or her regularly.

strategic decision [N-COUNT-U9] A **strategic decision** is a decision that is made for the purpose of improving one's situation.

supply and distribution channels [N-COUNT-U11] **Supply and distribution channels** are established patterns of commerce.

tax avoidance [N-UNCOUNT-U13] **Tax avoidance** is any activity done to avoid paying taxes.

tax brackets [N-COUNT-U13] **Tax brackets** are divisions based on income that are each required to pay a different rate of tax.

tax breaks [N-COUNT-U13] **Tax breaks** are discounts on taxes that are offered to encourage some desired behavior.

tax evasion [N-UNCOUNT-U13] **Tax evasion** is a crime involving the avoidance of paying taxes.

tedious [ADJ-U14] If something is **tedious**, it is repetitive and boring.

think twice [V-PHRASE-U4] To **think twice** is to reconsider a situation before acting due to concerns regarding potential failure or danger.

third party [N-COUNT-U14] A **third party** is someone other than the two principal parties in an agreement.

tighten [V-T-U6] To **tighten** something is to reduce its activity and flexibility.

tonal cues [N-COUNT-U10] **Tonal cues** are signals that are sent through changes in vocal pitch.

under-the-table payoff [N-PHRASE-U3] An **under-the-table payoff** is a bribe.

unforeseen [ADJ-U4] If something is **unforeseen**, it is not expected.

useful life [N-COUNT-U12] A product's **useful life** is the period of time in which it can be used.

utilities [N-COUNT-U1] **Utilities** are modern conveniences like running water, gas, and electricity.

variable cost [N-COUNT-U5] A **variable cost** is an expense that rises and falls with the volume of production.

variable overhead [N-UNCOUNT-U5] **Variable overheads** are costs such as utilities that rise and fall with the volume of production.

venture [N-COUNT-U11] A **venture** is an investment for the purpose of generating more income.

verbal cues [N-COUNT-U10] **Verbal cues** are signals that are sent through patterns in words.

vernacular [N-UNCOUNT-U10] **Vernacular** is common, everyday language.

viability [N-UNCOUNT-U11] **Viability** is the ability to survive and be successful.

working capital [N-UNCOUNT-U2] **Working capital** is assets minus liabilities.

worldwide trend [N-COUNT-U9] A **worldwide trend** is a pattern of behavior that is happening all over the world.

yardstick [N-COUNT-U6] A **yardstick** is a tool used to measure things.

Career Paths

Get the passport to a promising international career

www.careerpaths-esp.com

English for Specific Purposes

These books are designed for professionals, and students in vocational schools and colleges to help them develop the language skills they need to succeed in a professional work environment.

Express Publishing

For more information:
www.careerpaths-esp.com

- Accounting
- Agricultural Engineering
- Agriculture
- Air Force
- Architecture
- Art & Design
- Au Pair
- Automotive Industry
- Banking
- Beauty Salon
- Business English
- Call Centers
- Civil Aviation
- Civil Engineering
- Command & Control
- Computer Engineering
- Computing
- Construction I – Buildings
- Construction II – Roads & Highways
- Cooking
- Dental Hygienist
- Dentistry
- Elder Care
- Electrical Engineering
- Electrician
- Electronics
- Engineering
- Environmental Engineering
- Environmental Science
- Finance
- Firefighter
- Fishing & Seafood Industry
- Fitness Training
- Flight Attendant
- Food Service Industries
- Genetic Engineering
- Hotels & Catering
- Human Resources
- Industrial Engineering
- Information Technology
- Insurance
- Journalism
- Kindergarten Teacher
- Landscaping
- Law
- Logistics
- Management I
- Management II
- Marine Engineering
- MBA English
- Mechanical Engineering
- Mechanics
- Medical
- Medical Equipment Repair
- Merchant Navy
- Museum Management & Curatorship
- Natural Gas I
- Natural Gas II
- Natural Resources I – Forestry
- Natural Resources II – Mining
- Navy
- Nuclear Engineering
- Nursing
- Nutrition & Dietetics
- Paramedics
- Pet Care
- Petroleum I
- Petroleum II
- Physician Assistant
- Physiotherapy
- Plant Production
- Plumbing
- Police
- Psychology
- Public Relations
- Rail Transportation
- Real Estate
- Sales and Marketing
- Science
- Secretarial
- Security Personnel
- Software Engineering
- Sports
- TAXI Drivers
- Tourism
- Travel Agent
- University Studies
- Wireless Communications
- World Cup
- Worldwide Sports Events